Energy and the European Communities

Europa Publications Limited
18 Bedford Square, London, WC1B 3JN

© The David Davies Memorial Institute
of International Studies, 1977

ISBN: 0 905118 14 6

Printed and bound in England by
STAPLES PRINTERS LIMITED
at The Stanhope Press, Rochester, Kent.

Energy and the European Communities

N. J. D. Lucas

Published for The David Davies Memorial Institute
of International Studies
by
EUROPA PUBLICATIONS
LONDON

To Danièle
One of the last of the federalists.

Acknowledgements

This study was originally initiated by the David Davies Memorial Institute of International Studies, and I am most grateful for the help I received in preparing it, particularly from the Director, Miss Mary Sibthorp, whose remarkable tenacity and persistence have been invaluable.

I wish also to record how refreshingly open an administration is the Commission and to thank the many of its officers who gave me so generously of their time and who answered my questions so fully. If I do not thank them by name it is because I suspect that they would not always wish to be associated, even indirectly, with parts of my analysis and conclusions. My debt, nevertheless, is enormous.

Finally, I should like to thank Miss Esme Allen for typing the manuscript and bearing with my interminable revisions.

Contents

Foreword

Lord Thomson of Monifieth

This important book sets out to explore the history of Community energy policy, to analyse the Community decision-making process, to evaluate present policies and to make suggestions about future policies.

It is a timely book. Europe's continuing dependence on supplies of imported oil has grave implications for our economies and employment prospects. At the same time, there is a rising tide of concern throughout Europe about the implications of, and justification for, a large-scale commitment to nuclear energy, that apparent solution to our oil problems, and a growing if belated recognition of the appalling risks of proliferation posed by nuclear exports. These concerns about nuclear energy are legitimate, and thorough public debate would be wholly welcome.

Nigel Lucas has set himself an unusually challenging and complex task. He rises to that challenge convincingly. He displays a remarkable synthesis of skills in the diverse fields of energy policy, economic analysis, historical appreciation, and political and administrative analysis.

I should point out that I have two particular interests in this book. The first is as Chairman of the David Davies Memorial Institute of International Studies, which inspired its writing and which, amongst its objectives, seeks to promote a sane policy for the exploitation of natural resources. Secondly, I was a member of the European Commission during the period of which Nigel Lucas writes. As such, I bear my share of collective responsibility for the energy policy which he dissects so perceptively. Without seeking to shirk that responsibility, I am bound to say that the longer the debate in the Commission went on, the more concerned I became about the nuclear implications of the energy crisis, particularly the risks to international peace and stability from nuclear exports, and the risks to posterity arising from the legacy of nuclear waste.

One of the unnoticed virtues of the European Commission is that it is a much more open political society than most national administrations. The Commission has, I am glad to say, always welcomed constructive criticism, and I have no hesitation, both as a recent European Commissioner and as Chairman of the David Davies Memorial Institute, in expressing the hope that this book will be widely read, as it most certainly deserves to be.

Abbreviations

AEC	Atomic Energy Commission
AGIP	Agenzia Generale Italiana Petrole
ATIC	Association Technique de l'Importation
BWR	Boiling Light-Water-Cooled and Moderated Reactor
CAP	Common Agricultural Policy
COPENUR	Standing Committee on Uranium Enrichment
COREPER	Committee of Permanent Representatives
CREST	Committee for Research in Energy-Related Science and Technology
DCF	Discounted Cash Flow
EAEC	European Atomic Energy Community
ECE	Economic Commission for Europe
ECG	Energy Co-ordination Group
ECITO	European Central Inland Transport Organization
ECO	European Coal Organization
ECSC	European Coal and Steel Community
EDF	Electricité de France
EEC	European Economic Community
EIB	European Investment Bank
ENEL	Ente Nazionale per l'Energia Elettrica
EURATOM	European Atomic Energy Community
GEORG	Gemeinschaftsorganisation Ruhrkole
GW(e)	1,000 MW(e)
HTR	High-Temperature Reactor
IEA	International Energy Agency
LNG	Liquefied Natural Gas
LWR	Light-Water-Cooled and Moderated Reactor
MSP	Minimum Support Price
MTCE	Million Tons Coal Equivalent
MVA	Megavolt Amp
MW(e)	Megawatt electrical
NCB	National Coal Board
NPT	Non-Proliferation Treaty
OECD	Organization for Economic Co-operation and Development

OEEC   Organization for European Economic Co-operation
ORGEL   Organic Liquid-Cooled Reactor
PWR   Pressurized Light-Water-Cooled and Moderated
                   Reactor
SGHWR   Steam-Generating Heavy-Water Reactor
SNG   Substitute Natural Gas
SWU   Separative Work Units
UCPTE   Union for the Co-ordination of Production and
                   Transport of Electricity
UKAEA   United Kingdom Atomic Energy Authority
UNIPEDE International Union of Producers and Distributors of
                   Electricity

Note: References are listed at the end of each chapter. Reference numbers may appear more than once in the text.

Introduction

Energy is a fascinating subject; so is Europe. But the conjunction of circumstances is such as to make the attraction of energy in Europe quite irresistible.

Energy is of crucial economic significance. Although there is scope for substitution between fuels and to some extent between fuels and capital, and to some extent amongst activities using more or less fuel, in the end no economic system can survive without adequate supplies of energy. Many great industrial centres grew up around readily accessible sources of cheap energy which became uneconomic when vast reserves of oil were discovered in the Middle East. For Japan and Western Europe the fuel was coal, and these regions of the world now have the common problems of a declining indigenous coal industry and a heavy dependence on imported fuels. The industrial strength of the U.S.A. early in this century was based on its own resources of oil, but here again imports eventually became cheaper than home supplies. The changing reactions of the government of the U.S.A. to this state of affairs have appreciably influenced the course of energy policies elsewhere in the world. For these direct and indirect reasons it follows that as fuel is used less and less where it is found, so European energy policy has become more and more involved in foreign politics. The proliferation of thermonuclear weapons as a consequence of the commercial development of nuclear power is a new and even more serious entanglement of energy and foreign policy.

The energy industries are also simply a large and important part of the economies of Western Europe. About a quarter of all new investment in industry in the European Economic Community is intended to supply fuel or to convert a primary fuel into a secondary fuel, or into electricity or power. The energy supply industries in the Community directly employ about two million people and indirectly support all other activities. The availability of energy is an important determinant of the siting of today's industrial investment in manufacturing, and therefore of tomorrow's social and regional problems.

The provision of energy is also constrained by that other great modern preoccupation, the environment. The law of diminishing returns, personal experience and common sense suggest that, in general, the benefits of every additional piece of industrial development will be less than those from preceding development, whereas the recreational and agricultural value of the remaining land, of clear rivers and other aspects of a pleasant environment will be enhanced by scarcity. The provision and conversion of energy has many deleterious environmental consequences, including dereliction from coal mining, oil spills, air pollution, pollution of rivers and offshore waters, and disfigurement of the landscape by electricity generating plant, transmission lines and oil refineries. Environmental constraints and conflicts of land use already modify industrial and energy policy; their importance in restraining development, altering its character or diverting resources to alleviating its consequences will certainly increase.

In a slightly different category there are the radiation hazards of nuclear energy, the safety problems of reactors, and the possible restriction of civil liberties in an economy dependent on the handling of radioactive and fissile material.

The interrelationships of energy policy with these political, social, regional and environmental matters within a single nation are complicated; they are even more complicated when considered from within the EEC. Essentially this paper is concerned with the formation of policy within the EEC: the agents, their responsibilities, their objectives, and the mechanism of construction. To treat this subject without detailed consideration of the history of EEC energy policy, the problems already faced, the solutions devised and their consequences – such a treatment could only be anecdotal. The historical preamble therefore occupies over half of this paper.

The principal aims are:

to examine policy formulation within a highly technical sector and to determine if possible how political control operates in practice;

to examine the conflict between long-term planning, predicated on the technical characteristics of energy supply and on long-term political considerations, and the short-term requirements of politicians to satisfy their constituents.

The chapters which follow this introduction may appear francophobic. It is as well, therefore, to make it plain now that I believe the French intellectual tradition to be the most substantial contributor at present to any aim or leadership for Europe. This is because there is little political consensus among European states and little determination in the states with power; in the absence of these factors more subtle sources of coherent aims and leadership can operate.

After the visionary enthusiasm of the 1950s and the economic successes of the 1960s, which reflected well on the Community even if there was no substantial connection, the movement towards European integration appears to have faltered, if not to have reversed. Arguably the Community actually serves its finest purpose when times are bad, when it has no reflected economic glory in which to bask, but when it can, clumsily and imperfectly, contain the damage. The Community may not appear to be contributing much to the solution of the present economic problems of Western Europe, but things would be much worse if the spirit of European co-operation did not exist at all. European history is not short of examples of alternatives.

But be that as it may, the Community does exhibit great disarray. There is no obvious leadership or purpose, and many of the national governments are distracted by serious domestic troubles. The United Kingdom is preoccupied with one of the worst periods in its economic history. Italy has severe economic problems and even more serious political problems which threaten its always fragile national unity. Germany does not have political uncertainties of comparable magnitude and is indisputably the strongest economic power in Europe, but the pro-European image which she constantly projects is not borne out by certain specific actions and, more generally, by her reluctance to attempt to lead Community affairs. A partial explanation of this ambiguity is probably to be found in the German belief that the North Atlantic, and not Europe, is the region within which to construct new initiatives. This lack of conviction in the importance of the European grouping is not conducive to determined leadership. Allied to this is an aloof awareness that Germany alone of the member states could satisfactorily survive the destruction of the Community, and that, in energy, in particular she can always buy her way out of trouble with the products of her manufacturing industry.

France has the same problems as other European countries; certainly, her political base is not more stable. But she is sustained by her intellectual tradition and is ready to think ahead, formulate a policy, and make it known to and adopted by everyone concerned. She is ready to take political and technical risks; she is willing to recognize that European interests are not necessarily identical with those of the U.S.A. and are not necessarily advanced by falling in with American ideas. These are the indispensable qualities of leadership and if, as a result, the initiatives of the EEC have a curiously French look about them, and if the EEC energy policy is strongly influenced by French civil servants, then it is deserved.

Unfortunately, the risks the French take do not always come off, and there are reasons to believe that their diagnosis and treatment of energy policy are not the best. It is a thesis of this paper that indicative planning of energy supplies has a disastrous historical record and has damaged the growth of a common energy policy. The best one can do is to identify the likely nature of change and design institutions to cope with it. This form of planning for the future would fit well into the United Kingdom tradition of pragmatism. There is no reason why the United

Kingdom tradition should not succeed in Brussels, and by every measure it should be the more attractive to the real economic power of the Community. The energy policy, where solid, pragmatic opportunities for progress exist, is a good place to make a start.

I

History and Preoccupations of European Energy Policy

The history of energy in Europe since the end of the Second World War is an intricate development of relatively few themes; the whole is conveniently divided into several movements.

Roughly, from the end of the war to the mid-1950s was a time of recovery. There followed a short period of visions and a time of endeavour to 1967. From 1968 to the beginning of 1973 was an entr'acte, and since the British entry there has been a great deal of activity and little substantial achievement.

It is odd that energy policy, which has apparently been so unsuccessful, has frequently been presented as a reason or pretext for European integration. Part of the justification for going over some well-known ground in this chapter is to examine how energy policy was used to further the course of European integration and with what success, and how the course of European integration has in turn affected energy policy.

A. A Time of Recovery

The solidarity in production thus established will make it plain that war between France and Germany becomes not merely unthinkable but materially impossible. . . .   Robert Schuman,[1] 1950.

The Second World War demolished the established framework of energy supply in Europe. Before the war 90 per cent of primary energy came from coal; the war disrupted production and distribution. The traditional structure of exports from the coal producing countries, Germany, Poland and the United Kingdom, collapsed; indigenous mines were worked to the limit, equipment was not properly maintained, there was no new investment, unskilled and inefficient labour was drafted to the pits and in some cases forced labour was employed.

1

Collieries and coke ovens were destroyed by bombardment, sabotage and fighting.

In parts of Germany only one-fifth as much coal was being mined at the end of the war as at the beginning. In Belgium and the Netherlands between 30 and 40 per cent of production survived, 70 per cent in France and only 85 per cent even in the United Kingdom. Stocks of coal at the pitheads, which at the beginning of the war had been high as a consequence of the depression, were exhausted.[2]

The established structure of distribution suffered even more severely. Supplies everywhere were directed to the purposes of war; distribution of energy as gas was impeded by the destruction of plant for gasification; distribution as coal was impeded by the destruction of the railways and the chaotic dispersal of rolling stock as a result of military requisitioning.

As the war came to an end the armed forces undertook the distribution of what coal there was, but this procedure was not appropriate in peace time. After the war, therefore, an *ad hoc* intergovernmental institution known as the European Coal Organization (ECO) was formed, at the instigation of the U.S.A., and made responsible for allocating coal as fairly as possible among competing needs, and for apportioning among participating countries the scarce imports of coal and of materials and equipment for mining. Priority in the reconstruction of Europe was given to the production and distribution of coal, and the amount of coal available increased rapidly. By May 1947 the total production of coal in the states of the ECO had doubled in two years and in parts of Western Germany had almost tripled. Nevertheless, despite this statistical success, coal remained scarce and the harsh winter of 1946/47 caused terrible hardship on the continent of Europe.[2] It should remind us still how fundamental energy is to modern industrial society.

As an institution the ECO was a temporary response to an abnormal situation; many of its decisions were arbitrary and imposed in almost military fashion. During the two years of its life the European economies recovered rapidly and the ECO, designed essentially as an instrument of European reconstruction, was not thought an appropriate institution to continue the promotion of European co-operation. The ECO was nevertheless the first attempt by European states to deal with the supply and distribution of energy within Europe as a whole; it made manifest a discontinuous change in the perception of energy supply by governments; by force of circumstances the problem of supplying energy was explored within the space of Europe. A new perception of transport was similarly forced on governments and manifested in the European Central Inland Transport Organization (ECITO), an institution much like the ECO.[3]

In May 1947 the tasks of the ECO and the ECITO were taken over by a new regional commission of the Economic and Social Council of the United Nations – the Economic Commission for Europe (ECE). The new resolve of the European governments to retain responsibility for the co-ordinated development of transport was expressed by establishing within the ECE an Inland Transport Committee with extensive interests in international regulation and common transport policy. The new European perception of energy supply had no such immediate consequence, probably because the sector offers rather less scope for real progress through international regulation.

A year later, in May 1948, the Organization for European Economic Co-operation (OEEC) was established. A condition of Marshall aid was closer collaboration among the states of Europe, and the OEEC was intended to assist in this effort by expanding production, increasing productivity, liberalizing intra-European trade and possibly harmonizing Western European monetary policy. The Council of the OEEC set up permanent committees for coal, electricity and oil. The last of these committees was to do good work in identifying the principal future changes in European energy supply, deducing the consequences and suggesting some of the remedies. The other energy committees have left less of a mark.

One of the last acts of the ECO was to agree on targets for the production of coal in the constituent countries and in Western Germany for the next four years to 1951. The objective of the plans was to produce as much coal as before the war and to keep imports of oil as low as possible in order to preserve foreign exchange; a shortage of dollars was a most important constraint on European affairs at that time.

In the United Kingdom, France and Western Germany ambitious plans were designed for the future of the industry in the long-term; the French plan was drafted by Jean Monnet, later an important actor in European integration. In the United Kingdom and France the powers necessary to make these targets of practical significance were acquired by nationalization of the coal mining industries; in Western Germany, control of the coal industry lay with the Allies in the International Ruhr Authority. The plans were on the whole successful; up to 1948 the domestic production of coal had to be supplemented by enormous imports from America; after 1948 the total quantity of imports began to fall and the principal source of imports shifted across the Atlantic to Poland. Eventually only the imports of coking coal from the U.S.A. remained, and these, an innovation after the war, have persisted ever since.

By 1950 the German economy had revived to such an extent that the Allies could no longer plausibly expect to exert control over the German coal and steel industries through the International Ruhr Authority.

France, however, would not accept that restrictions be entirely removed. Robert Schuman therefore proposed a common market in coal and steel that would make 'war between France and Germany . . . not merely unthinkable but materially impossible'. At the time coal and steel were thought of as the commanding heights of the economy and the basis of military might. In fact, the coal industry was poised for decline and even steel was to lose something of its pre-eminence among structural materials. But this was not critical; the enduring objectives were reconciliation and a new political order.

The Schuman plan and the Treaty of Paris creating the European Coal and Steel Community (ECSC) were drafted principally by Jean Monnet, at that time head of the French *Commissariat du Plan*. The institutional apparatus was complex for its limited purpose and was no doubt designed as a model for things to come. Under the ECSC Treaty the dialogue between the Commission and the Council, which was to be the really original institutional feature of the later EEC Treaty, already existed, but only in embryo. The executive, the contemporary equivalent of the Commission, was known as the High Authority, and bore a great deal of the responsibility for implementing the Treaty, although the Council of Ministers was required to endorse especially important decisions. Compelled by the real fear of war the member states agreed to a supranationalist quality that they eschewed in the later Communities; the High Authority was given statutory powers over the national economies and was financed independently by a levy on the coal and steel producing industries. With prompting from the U.S.A. when negotiations faltered, the Treaty of Paris was signed in April 1951; Monnet was appointed as the first President. The United Kingdom would not concede powers to an authority that was 'utterly undemocratic and responsible to nobody', and declined to join.

The expectations of the Community were mainly political; France established its authority and moral leadership on continental Western Europe, retained indirectly some control over the expanding German steel industry, and obtained access to German coke and coal. Germany recovered essential control over its basic industries and achieved political respectability. But there were economic expectations as well; the ECSC was devised as a customs union, and a body of economic theory suggested that industry would become more efficient because of specialization prompted by free trade, increased competition and larger markets. There were also misgivings: countries that were favourably endowed with resources resented the measures proposed against cartels, and they were supported by some economists who argued that the cartels gave stability to the industries; countries poorly endowed with resources were afraid that their own industries would not survive competition.

The High Authority was to organize this union, do what it could to alleviate the hardship in areas dependent on non-competitive coal mining, and attempt to distribute benefits fairly. The ECSC was created at a propitious time; coal was still scarce, but except in a few areas output was rising fast and economies were growing rapidly. The High Authority was in the happy position of presiding over the distribution of an expanding resource in strong demand. Its best years were during the boom of 1955 to 1957. It is a theme of this paper that common policies do best in such an environment. There is then something for everyone; the countries possessing the resource benefit from the revenue obtained by producing more and selling into foreign markets to which home production no longer has privileged access; countries with poor resources benefit from lower-cost foreign production. There are naturally problems in distributing the benefits and alleviating hardship, but for curious psychological reasons they are more easily solved than the reciprocal problems of distributing the costs of protecting contracting industries.

In the beginning the preoccupation of the ECSC in the market-place was to make sure coal was available on non-discriminatory terms and that prices were stable and reasonable; the preoccupation in production was to continue, as rapidly as possible, the expansion of an industry still underinvested and poorly maintained.

At the time of the Treaty both the cost of mining coal and the price at which it was sold differed widely between the six countries. The methods which governments used to control prices also differed, and a variety of ingeniously disguised quantitative restrictions operated. In Germany the government set maximum prices for each coalfield and lignite mine. In France, first the government decided the general level of prices, then the *Charbonnages de France* calculated average prices for the various coalfields, and finally on this basis the prices for different grades of coal were fixed. In the Netherlands the government fixed 'delivered prices' which were identical everywhere in the country for a given grade of coal, whether indigenous or imported. In Italy a complex system operated in which the price of imports (the main source of energy) were fixed essentially as cost plus a defined profit. Prices were also controlled in Belgium and Luxembourg.

The Treaty of Paris foresaw a preparatory period, before the common markets were established, during which member states would rescind, as requested by the High Authority, all national regulations impeding the movements of coal, iron ore and scrap. Import and export duties, quantitative restrictions on imports and exports, subsidies, financial preferences and restrictions on the provision of foreign exchange for purchase of imports, dual pricing systems and discriminatory practices in transport were largely abolished. The preparatory period

5

ended on 10 February 1953, when a common market in these goods was created. After that date the High Authority became truly supranational; it exercised powers which formerly were those of national governments and which were assigned to it by the six member states of the Community. These powers included the right to fix prices. The High Authority chose to take advantage of that power immediately in an effort to halt the continual rise in prices of coal products that had persisted since the end of the war; this increase was widely expected to continue because of the prevailing difficulty in obtaining certain types of coal and the high price of coal imported from America. Maximum prices for coal were therefore fixed to avoid prices hardening. The mechanism was to fix in the principal coal fields:

(a) an upper limit on price for each type of coal, being a weighted average of prices of the various grades;

(b) a ceiling for each type of coal above which no grade could be sold;

(c) a ceiling price for certain grades, most importantly blast furnace coke.

The chief problem, evidently, was to calculate the average and ceiling prices. The High Authority was anxious to avoid abrupt changes that would do more harm than good, but it reflected philosophically that considerable protection existed naturally for local coal because the value of coal was relatively small compared to its weight, so that the price of coal increased rapidly over the pithead price as it was transported. This is still true today, but it applied even more strongly with the contemporary transport system. The High Authority therefore fixed prices rather low, which procedure had the enormous ancillary benefit of permitting the High Authority to point the following year to a fall in coal prices as evidence of the success of the common market. To avoid too dramatic a change certain restrictive practices were tolerated temporarily; they remained in force under constant control of the High Authority and were to be abolished progressively. A system of compensation was also introduced (as laid down in the Treaty) to help Belgian and Italian coal mining industries to adapt progressively to the new conditions.

Price control by the High Authority was controversial from the beginning; oddly, the coal producing countries were at first broadly happy with it and the consuming countries tended to be more disconsolate, suggesting that pressure on prices was really downwards. The High Authority insisted, with justification, that if it did not control prices then prices would be determined by the cartels in the Ruhr basin and in the collieries of the Nord and Pas-de-Calais coalfields. When the High Authority reviewed its price-fixing scheme in March 1954 it compromised by removing control from all fields other than those of the Ruhr basin and the Nord and Pas-de-Calais. The old price level was maintained in the French fields and actually reduced in the Ruhr. The following year (1955/56) the High Authority abolished price control in the French fields but retained the maximum price in the Ruhr at the same level as the preceding year; it did this because it regarded the selling system in the Ruhr as a restriction on genuine competition in the common market. It was true that the Ruhr coal barons operated a blatant cartel; all coal produced in the Ruhr was sold by a single sales organization, enjoying the name *Gemeinschaftsorganisation Ruhrkole*, sinister to non-Germanophones, but affectionately known as GEORG.

However, about this time the High Authority launched an attack on all coal cartels in Germany, Belgium and France. A fight inevitably developed over the French and German monopoly agencies. Against GEORG the French fielded the *Association Technique de l'Importation* (ATIC). In 1952 ATIC was the sole purchaser of imported coal in France. The French Government refused to accept reorganization of ATIC without changes in GEORG; they argued that GEORG controlled half of the Community coal output and that the only defence the French consumer could erect against such a cartel was a monopoly purchasing organization. There is some merit in this argument, but it conflicts with France's present refusal to contemplate a monopoly purchasing agency for oil against the OPEC selling cartel.

Eventually the High Authority obtained changes in both organizations which satisfied itself and the French and German Governments. The High Authority refused to allow either a single organization to continue selling in the Ruhr or two organizations, but it was willing to authorize three selling agencies; the Ruhr enterprises agreed to this proposal. It must be said to the credit of the German Government that, faithful to its free enterprise principles, it persistently supported the High Authority in its efforts to create a common market in coal, counter to the interests of powerful groups in Germany including businessmen, trade unionists and politicians from all parties. A good deal of German opinion saw the whole business of the ECSC as a French plot to distribute German resources to its neighbour; there was considerable truth in that and it is easy enough to see how the matter could be exaggerated; later, however, this resistance began to carry some weight.

But for the moment demolition of GEORG diminished the principal argument for price control in the Ruhr. The ECSC Consultative Committee disliked price fixing in general, but thought that if it were to be applied in the Ruhr it should hold everywhere; by this time the pressure on prices was upwards and the Ruhr owners were protesting strongly at price controls. Eventually, during 1955/56, the High Authority gave up price control in the Ruhr. Interestingly, the Executive went against the view of the Council of Ministers who voted three to two for maximum prices, with one abstention; although there was not a majority in favour and although the Council was only asked for an opinion, the incident illustrates the supranational powers of the High Authority and its willingness, at the time, to use them.

The second principal preoccupation of the High Authority was to assist the increase in production of coal. The coal industry was still suffering from the effects of the war, exacerbated by the cartels which had assured high prices and adequate returns for inefficient producers and removed the incentives for new investment. Partly no doubt because of the efforts of the High Authority, but mainly because of strong demand, the production of coal grew steadily until 1957. Unfortunately for the coal industry the total demand for energy increased still faster and the industry simply could not keep pace; oil was imported to make up the deficiency, with no immediate ill effect on the coal industry. But 1957 was a turning point; although the industrial recession, coupled with two mild winters, caused the total demand for energy to level off, the imports of oil continued to grow at much the same rate. Stocks of coal at the pitheads increased dramatically, even though production fell. Until 1957 oil had been seen as a supplementary fuel; thereafter perceptions changed.

Before the war oil was quantitatively of little importance in the economies of Western Europe; in 1938 it contributed about 8 per cent of the total consumption of primary energy in Western Europe, as opposed to 20 per cent in the world as a whole. But the events of that period were important, because it was then that the general principles determing the attitude of the national governments to the oil companies were formed; the divergent tendencies in the main European powers which dog energy policy today date back to well before the last war.

The oil industry was, and largely still is, an Anglo-Saxon monopoly. Because of its considerable petroleum reserves and because of many favourable aspects of the entrepreneurial climate, the U.S.A. quickly dominated the early world oil industry. The United Kingdom recognized that this state of affairs was strategically intolerable, and so gave the Anglo-Persian Oil Company (now British Petroleum) the benefit of its support and economic favours in those regions of the world where the British military and political presence was effective. Since these regions included the Middle East, the Anglo-Persian Oil Company flourished and obtained control of extensive oil reserves. The Anglo-Persian Oil Company, and later BP, still remained an independent private enterprise which, though having government-appointed members on its board, formulated its own policies with no formal government control. The relationship of Shell with the Netherlands and the United Kingdom had similar qualities, although it lacked the direct government stake.

France was slow to break into the industry. It eventually did so by acquiring a one-quarter share in the Turkish Petroleum Company as a result of the Versailles Peace Treaty. Faced with the problem of disposing of this oil with no existing infrastructure of supply and use, the French decided to impose a solution from above through government-controlled companies (*Compagnie Française des Pétroles* and *Compagnie Française de Raffinage*) and government control of the market by detailed regulation. Italy tried to imitate France's example through its own state oil company, AGIP (*Azienda Generale Italiana Petrole*), but she was much less successful, largely because she did not have access to oil reserves of her own. Italy did establish, however, a basis of regulations. Already, therefore, there existed the seeds of the different attitudes towards the oil companies, the consequences of which would later be such a problem: the connivance of the United Kingdom and the Netherlands, the detailed control of France and Italy, and the comparatively disinterested and free-market attitudes of Germany.

Because of their poor representation in the industry, the countries of continental Europe, with some exceptions, were slightly antagonistic to oil and deliberately attempted to reduce the demand for imported oil by using substitutes wherever possible. For example, plants were built in Germany before and during the war to make synthetic liquid fuels from coal; they were not strikingly successful. Alcohol, benzol and tar oil were also common substitutes for petroleum products.

Up to 1939 and immediately after the war the oil industry built refineries near the sources of crude oil and exported refined products to Europe; demand in Europe at that time was not sufficient to permit the economies of scale that were technically possible in the refining of oil, and it was more convenient to transport oil as products than as crude. The exception to this generalization was France, which insisted as part of its system of regulation that most oil should be imported as crude and refined in France, despite the economic penalty. Eventually, in order to reduce the foreign exchange cost of oil, other European governments tried to cajole and bully the oil companies into building refineries in Europe by offering financial inducements and by threatening to give preferences to imports of crude oil, thereby excluding companies who had not built refinery capacity in Europe. As it happened, these objectives of governments coincided with changes in the economic structure of the oil industry which shifted the economic advantage to European refineries. Both companies and governments therefore stood to benefit from a new strategy. By 1950 the first large European oil refineries were in operation, at Fawley, Pernis in the Netherlands and Marseilles.[4]

It is interesting to compare, in the reports of the oil committee of the OEEC, the contemporary perception of how the oil industry would

9

develop and the actual outcome. The oil committee had been instructed by the Council of the OEEC in July 1949 to examine the long-term refinery plans of the industry and to draw up a programme of co-ordinated construction and expansion of refineries in Western Europe. It represented a means whereby the member states of the OEEC could keep track of the powerful, mainly American, oil companies at a time when these companies were formulating plans for the supply of oil to Europe whose effects would persist for a considerable time.

The growth of the oil refining industry was extraordinarily rapid and took even the oil committee by surprise; in 1948 the throughput of crude oil in refineries in OEEC countries was 19.5 million tons, in 1955 it was 103 million tons. The reports of the oil committee in 1949, 1951 and 1953 persistently underestimated the rate of growth by a large amount.

Concurrently with the creation of a European refining industry, the United Kingdom Government put considerable pressure on the oil companies to reduce prices of crude oil and to substitute crude from sterling areas for crude from dollar areas. Some pressure also came from other European governments, but at the time they were weak and ineffective. The most effective influence came undoubtedly from the U.S.A., prompted by the Economic Co-operation Administration, which in using American money to buy oil for the purpose of the Marshall Plan concluded that the oil companies were discriminating against Europeans.[5] Essentially, the low-cost crude from the Middle East was sold at the price of high-cost crude from the U.S.A., which had come the much longer journey across the Atlantic. This kept prices high and removed the incentive to expand production from low-cost areas. In 1950 the oil companies agreed to dismantle the formal connection of the price of crude in Europe to the prices posted in the Gulf States; as a result prices dropped a little, but they were still well above cost. In practice the price of Middle Eastern crude continued to be tied to that of U.S. crude.

As the economies of the European states recovered they undertook a comprehensive examination of the practice of pricing oil within a special study group of the ECE; the study was published in March 1955 as *The Price of Oil in Western Europe*.[6] The study group set out to determine whether the prices for crude and petroleum products charged in Western Europe were fair and just; it concluded that no clear answer was possible because the usual measures of fair prices were meaningless given the complexity of the world oil industry; the work did, however, provide a detailed explanation of the costs of operations in the oil industry, their relationship, and the conflicting interests and forces influencing prices. The study group argued that the economics of petroleum could only be understood by examining the related operations in all parts of the world; it therefore analysed the influence of the U.S. domestic oil business on the international market and the consequences of the prevailing structure of ownership of the industry; although it avoided the question of fair prices, it did conclude that there was no compelling reason to tie the price of Middle Eastern crude to that of U.S. crude; it predicted also that prices in Europe would eventually drop because of a large potential oversupply at low cost. This remarkable report was by far the most perspicacious of the crop of visionary documents produced between 1955 and 1957; it had considerable influence on the formation of national attitudes to oil company affairs and oil policy, but its significance for European integration was either ignored or overlooked.

It is an excellent example of what can be done when people really try to assess how the future might differ from the present, rather than trying to prove it will be the way they would like it to be and justifying that proof by forecasts of future use given with spurious accuracy.

There is apparently a conflict between the conclusion here that the future importance of oil was distinguished in 1955 and the earlier conclusion that it was not until 1957 that oil was perceived other than as a supplementary fuel. The explanation for the conflict is, oddly enough, the Suez crisis of 1956. In 1955 the Suez canal appeared vital to the energy supply of Europe; that year it carried 69 million tons of oil. By far the most important consequence of the closure of the canal after the 1956 war in the Middle East was to delay the general understanding that Europe was moving from a period of scarce, expensive energy to a period of falling prices and abundant fuel. It also gave a quite unwarranted and ill-timed stimulus to nuclear energy, as we shall discuss later.

B. A Time of Visions

The United States of Europe, means: a federal power linked to the peaceful exploitation of Atomic Energy.   Jean Monnet,[7] 1955

The middle 1950s was a time when, simultaneously, the form of European integration was defined and the imminence of profound changes in the traditional structure of European energy was divined. The interdependence of political change and change in energy supply is evident in M. Monnet's vision of a Europe politically united, its industries invigorated by nuclear energy, and more generally in the persistent attempts to work energy into the institutional structure of the political union.

The years following the creation of the ECSC had been disappointing for enthusiasts of European integration; various initiatives aimed more or less directly at political union had failed. M. Monnet, impatient at

11

the delays in bringing other economic activities under international control, resigned from the ECSC to work full time for European integration through his 'Action Committee for the United States of Europe', an informal organization of political and trade union leaders obliged to promote the Committee's conclusions in their home countries. This Committee eventually had substantial influence on the early affairs of Euratom. Before leaving his post as President of the High Authority, Monnet nurtured within the ECSC the '*Relance Européenne*'; the ECSC was the pivot of the *Relance*; it had provided a supranational experience; its Assembly of members from national Parliaments fostered ideas of integration; and it provided, in its administration, a base for operations.[8] The material manifestation of the *Relance* was the memorandum submitted by the Benelux governments to the meeting of Foreign Ministers assembled at Messina to choose a successor for M. Monnet as President of the High Authority. The memorandum argued that European unity could only be achieved by economic integration entered into not only for its intrinsic benefits, but for political motives, and inspired ultimately by the ideal of political union; it proposed 'horizontal economic integration' through a common market and 'vertical economic integration' through joint action on conventional energy, atomic energy and transport. The Ministers agreed on a resolution which adopted the objectives of the Benelux programme and proposed procedures for implementing them. The resolution from the Messina conference[9] was much concerned with energy; of the three specific aims cited for European action, one was 'the development of exchange of gas and electric power, and a reduction of their cost, through co-ordination of the production and consumption of power and the formulation of a joint policy'; and a second was 'the creation of a joint organization having the responsibilities and the facilities for ensuring the development of atomic energy for peaceful purposes'.

The Ministers also agreed to appoint an inter-governmental committee, working under the direction of Paul-Henri Spaak, a fervent partisan of European unity, to study the problems raised by the new proposals and prepare drafts of treaties or agreements. The Committee established four Commissions of experts to examine:

 (i) the general common market;
 (ii) conventional energy;
(iii) atomic energy;
(iv) transport.

The Commissions were to outline the objectives of economic integration in each sector and design means of obtaining them. The Committee was to be helped by experts from ECSC, OEEC, the Council of Europe and the European Conference of Transport Ministers. The United

Kingdom was invited to attend the Committee's meetings, ostensibly because of Britain's membership of the Western European Union and her associate membership of the ECSC. However, Britain was hostile to both Communities; in particular, within Euratom the United Kingdom:

(i) stood to lose its monopoly of atomic expertise in Europe;

(ii) stood to lose its preferential access to uranium supplies from Canada, because of the proposal to establish a supranational uranium supply agency with an option on all uranium supplies.

Matters came to a head at a meeting of the Foreign Ministers in Brussels in February 1956, when M. Spaak presented an interim report on the Committee's work. As a public demonstration of its complete lack of interest in the atomic energy community, the United Kingdom chose to argue that the proposed European Community was incompatible with an international agency that the OEEC was trying to organize.[10] After a stormy session the United Kingdom took no further effective part in discussions.

It had been known since December 1955, when M. Spaak reported to the Council of Europe, that the *Relance* Committee had dropped proposals for new international organizations in transport and energy, but was continuing to prepare proposals for Euratom and the Common Market. After the interim report in February, the final report was published in April 1956[11] and submitted to the Council of Ministers in Paris the following month. The report is in three parts dealing with the Common Market, Euratom and sectors where urgent action was needed; the first among these was energy.

Nowadays it is fashionable to be sceptical about the extent to which science and technology outside a proper economic and political framework can themselves solve the problems of society. It therefore needs extensive quotation to convey the brightness of the vision of a new Europe founded on political union and atomic energy, and how simply the two were related. The U.S.A. was at last to be challenged, both in its political weight and in the access to cheap energy on which its industrial supremacy was thought to depend. The foreword of the *Relance* Committee, after drawing attention to the dominant position of the U.S.A. in almost every industrial and commercial activity and emphasizing the continuous relative decline of European influence, industrial power, productive capacity and overseas resource base, goes on:

> Europe as it stands cannot use the most powerful technological methods and above all it cannot compete with the U.S.A. in its understanding, mobilization and use of atomic energy. None of our countries is capable of the enormous effort in research and development and fundamental investments to stimulate the technical revolution promised by the atomic

age. . . . In a few years the atomic revolution will burst the archaic character of our economic structures. That is why in choosing to begin with the unification of Europe in the economic domain the six Ministers of Foreign Affairs gathered at Messina have stressed these two essential relationships: putting atomic industry in common and creating a general common market.[12]

Even in the introduction to the chapter on the common market, the commercial revolution is compared to the atomic revolution, rather than the reverse.

'Just as atomic energy gives greater freedom in siting industries, the common market will have its full effect in the management of affairs and the quality of men: the pooling of resources will assure equality of opportunity.' The introduction to the Euratom chapter is lyrical: 'The power of the atom was brusquely revealed to the world in a terrifying form. Ten years later it appears as the essential resource for the eventual development and renewal of production and the progress of peaceful works.'

A great sense of urgency runs through the report; a new technical revolution is coming; if Europe does not act to make up ground lost to the U.S.A., then its future will be compromised. The U.S.A. is evaluating prototypes of 30 different types of reactor, but Europe's energy is expensive; it is for Europe, much more than for the U.S.A., that the creation of this new source is an 'imperious necessity'.[13] The Spaak report proposed to establish in Euratom a common organization which would not only promote the formation and rapid growth of the nuclear industry but which would help with the transition of the whole economy from a coal to a nuclear base. The functions of the organization would be:

   research, development, and dissemination of knowledge;

   to establish common standards of safety in nuclear affairs;

   to facilitate investment;

   to promote security in supply of nuclear fuel and ensure equality of access;

   to assure a common market in all related materials, equipment and personnel.

The final chapter of the Spaak report is about specific sectors of the economy where urgent action in vertical integration is required. The first of these is energy; the introductory logic is particularly interesting. It is argued that the manufacture, transport and distribution of gas and electricity differ technically and economically from traffic in most manufactured goods. The reason for this is that, at the time, the electricity supply industry and coal-based gas industry were made up of relatively small organizations enjoying effective monopoly within most of their area of operation; the usual concept of competition did not apply and evidently could not be introduced. Therefore it was not thought possible to establish immediately a common market of the sort built up for coal within the ECSC.

Some sort of action was, however, recognized as urgent. Energy in Europe was dear and looked like getting continually more so. Supplies and prices were uncertain. The investments necessary to improve the industries were expensive and would not be working and producing adequate returns for several years after they were begun. Nuclear energy would be low cost, but as a consequence would threaten to compromise the viability of investment on conventional sources. A guide was therefore thought necessary to the amount of investment in conventional sources which would be required before the imminent transition to nuclear energy; the guide would be based on an assessment of available resources and future needs; it would recommend the most suitable long-term investment programme, detect obstacles to that programme, and advise on their removal.

This undertaking was not felt to justify a new institution, nor was it felt an appropriate activity for the EEC; it was suggested, therefore, that the responsibility should be assigned to the ECSC in collaboration with the Council and a special consultative committee. It was not proposed to give the ECSC powers of decision in these matters, but simply a watching brief. This was not unreasonable for the function proposed at that time, because both the gas and electricity supply industries depended almost exclusively on the coal industry for their feedstock; the ECSC therefore understood the gas and electricity industry and was competent to assume the responsibility given to it.

In the general matter of energy policy the experts of the *Relance* Commission on conventional energy agreed that there were several fundamental decisions that the Community had to make. These were, firstly, the preference to be accorded to low cost and security of supply; secondly, the relative importance to be given to present and future needs; thirdly, how to meet peak demands. Discrepancies between the policies adopted by different countries could distort competition within the Community and could prejudice the chances of reaching the best solution for the Community as a whole.

The report was adopted by the governments of the six in Venice in June 1956, as a basis for final proposals. A new Intergovernmental Committee was formed, chaired again by Spaak, which drafted the Treaties of Rome setting up the European Economic Community and the European Atomic Energy Community. The final drafts were completed in March 1957 and signed in Rome the same month; they came into force on 1 January 1958. Neither of the Treaties of Rome contains a single word about energy policy.

There are four related aspects of the part played by energy in these early days of European integration which, with hindsight, are interesting. First, why was energy policy ignored in the Treaties of Rome after being an important feature of the *Relance*; second, to what extent were the fundamental principles of energy policy accurately identified in the Spaak report; third, why the lack of concern with hydrocarbons, incredible in view of later events; and fourth, to what extent, underneath the rhetoric, was the nuclear vision really believed?

The absence, in the end, of a single word about energy policy in the Treaties of Rome is sometimes offered as a partial explanation of the difficulties later experienced in constructing a common policy.[14] Not only do the Treaties contain no provisions for a common policy, but by distributing the responsibilities among the three executives they almost ensured that no material progress should be made. The reasons for this absence are simple enough.

Energy policy as presented in the Spaak report did not then have the significance that it has since developed. Now, Europe is completely dependent for an adequate supply of energy on decisions taken elsewhere by non-Europeans; energy is a political matter of the greatest importance; in the Spaak report it was seen principally as just another manufactured good, with a curious economic structure presenting special problems which did not merit another institution, which were not capable of solution within the existing institutions, but which in any case were not important because fairly soon the basic energy source of the Community would be nuclear. The argument would have been unsound even if nuclear energy had lived up to expectations; the efficient distribution of electricity and use of nuclear power stations would have required an integrated European electricity transmission and distribution network which none of the Community institutions could have promoted effectively. But this technical point apart, and given the interpretation of the present and the vision of the future apparently adopted by the *Relance* Committee, the energy sector seemed to be reasonably well covered by the ECSC and Euratom. Only two fuels were of any consequence, coal and nuclear. Nuclear fuel, the energy of the future, was to be looked after in Euratom; coal and the associated coal conversion industries supplying electricity and gas could be looked after in the ECSC. Finally, the political advantage lay in being seen to lead Europe to the nuclear age. There is no doubt that political objectives dominated the priorities of the Treaties of Rome; the spirit of the time was contained in Hallstein's famous epigram: 'the Communities are in politics, not business'.

The second matter of interest arising from the Spaak report is the accuracy with which the fundamental questions of principle in energy policy were perceived and expressed. The choice between cost and security was strongly emphasized and did indeed prove to be the principal theme of Community energy policy, although at times strenuous effort would be made to pretend otherwise. The experts must have had in mind the possibility of a dependence on oil imports into European markets so excessive as to inhibit free conduct of foreign policy and to threaten security, but no attempt was made to anticipate the consequences on the structure of Community institutions.

The second choice, between present and future, is inevitably a part of any decision to invest; the essence of investment is to forego present benefits for future benefits. Far from being a fundamental choice of energy policy, it appears at first sight little more than an empty generalization. Nevertheless, the problem of assessing the future benefits of a decision is particularly acute in energy; capital investments take a long time to bring on stream and far longer to cover their costs; their success depends on assumptions which are often uncertain. It is the familiar paradox that we need a long-term policy because only then is it possible to invest confidently and consistently but, on the other hand, because we cannot foresee the future we cannot create an appropriate long-term policy without running the risk of prejudicing future options. A long-term policy is, then, both essential and impossible. To some extent the future conditions necessary for the success of a policy can be created by resolute prosecution of that policy; for example, more active development of nuclear energy in the 1960s in the face of adverse economic conditions might have created a stronger nuclear industry that could have solved the technical problems involved and produced nuclear materials, constructed nuclear reactors and generated electricity at costs so low as to have justified the initiative. Arguments like this are difficult to assess, but they have a real chance of being true. It is, therefore, particularly difficult in energy policy to evaluate the consequences of decisions over a period of time comparable to the duration of the effect of the decision. This paradox has never been satisfactorily resolved and is a second important theme of community energy policy. It is, of course, not always noticeable, in the manner of the dog that did not bark in the night. Questions of this sort were almost certainly in the minds of the experts who drafted the generalization that actually appeared in the Spaak report, and they deserve the credit for distinguishing this second important theme.

The last choice, of the means of meeting peak demand, is a technical consideration which no doubt occupied the time of many managers of the small independent gas and electricity supply industries which existed in that period and which had nothing to fall back on in times of peak demand but their own small resources. With hindsight, however, it scarcely seems of the same consequence as the preceding pair.

The experts therefore appear to have identified in general terms the

17

principles of energy policy. By contrast, the perception of the future in practice was disastrously wrong; there is almost no discussion of hydro-carbons in the Spaak report and a devout faith in nuclear energy. To understand why this was so requires that we first look elsewhere. The evolution of the institutions of Europe is only one melody in the counterpoint; the other is the new perception of energy in Europe.

One of the men who most influenced this perception was M. Louis Armand. He had been chairman of the *Société Nationale des Chemins de fer Français*; he became chairman of the Industrial Equipment Committee of the French Atomic Energy Commissariat and energy consultant to the OEEC. In this last capacity M. Armand wrote a report on the energy economy of Western Europe,[15] which was published just before the Spaak Committee began work; as a result he was appointed chairman of the Commission of Experts on Nuclear Energy, and he later became the first President of the Euratom Commission. In the interval between the publication of the Spaak report and the signing of the Rome Treaties he wrote, with two others, a *Target for Euratom*[16] which determined the early years of that institution and whose influence on policy in the EEC can, on some interpretations, be detected still.

Armand's first report was published in July 1955, three months after *The Price of Oil in Western Europe*;[6] the principal thesis was that Western Europe was passing from an era characterized by shortage of a single fuel to a new era of competition between fuels. Armand reviewed the extensive resources of uranium fuel, stressed the convenience of transmission and distribution as electricity, and argued that nuclear costs should soon be competitive; he concluded that early development of this energy source was essential to halt the economic decline of Europe and recommended a co-operative effort in building and financing nuclear energy that would be justified by technical, economic and political reasons.

In his report to the OEEC Armand recommended that a group of experts be gathered to examine the whole problem of energy in Western Europe and particularly the role of nuclear energy; the recommendation was accepted and a Commission was created, chaired by the distinguished United Kingdom scientist, Sir Harold Hartley. The Commission published its report in May 1956,[17] just after the report of the *Relance* Committee. The Commission estimated that energy use in the 18 OEEC countries would increase to between 1,100 and 1,300 MTCE by 1975 and that indigenous production would be no more than 755 MTCE; the remainder would have to come from imports of coal or oil and from nuclear power. The Commission made tentative estimates of the amount of energy that might be obtained from nuclear fuels by extending to other member countries predictions made for the United Kingdom; the results are not clearly expressed in the report but quoted as percentages of numbers that are themselves not clearly defined, and at least two separate and distinct expressions are apparently contradictory. The confusion almost certainly arose from the presence on the Committee of enthusiasts and sceptics whose difference of opinion had to be obscured. The most telling evaluation of nuclear power is the qualitative assessment which warns against 'the fanciful hope' placed in it by the public. Although the Committee expected that nuclear power would eventually be of the greatest importance, they foresaw that exploitation of this form of energy would pose difficult and unexpected problems. They predicted also that coal would remain the principal fuel in Europe for many years and they argued that for too long the coal industry had been seen as static and even declining; they attributed the currency of this opinion originally to the uncertainty of the period between the wars that prevented long-term investment, and recently to the widespread conviction that nuclear energy would soon replace coal. The Commission thought this conviction misplaced and advocated long-term investment in the coal industry, the creation of better working conditions, the adoption of better working methods, modernization and higher salaries.

The Hartley report had great merit; it clearly foresaw the transition from a self-sufficient or energy exporting region to a region heavily dependent on imports, and it correctly described the problems that this would bring, including the strategic dependence. It was also commendably sceptical about nuclear energy, but in common with most other contemporary works the study failed to predict the astonishing penetration of European markets by petroleum. Nevertheless, energy policy in the EEC might have evolved more fruitfully if the perception of the Hartley report, for all its faults, had been current within the European movement. In fact it appears to have had little effect on the preparation for the EEC and Euratom. Less well known than the Hartley report, but in some ways a more interesting document, is another OEEC paper published later that year.[18] This paper, entitled *Oil – the outlook for Europe*, was produced by the Oil Committee of the OEEC and undertook to examine in detail the position of oil in Europe's energy supply within the context of the broader study by the Commission for Energy. The Oil Committee was clear about its assessment of the commercial competitiveness of nuclear energy.

> In general, our view is that the oil requirements are likely to lie nearer the Commission's maximum figure than to the minimum, and we have therefore accepted this maximum figure as the most useful guide, despite recent unofficial statements that nuclear energy may make a greater contribution during the period under review than suggested in the report of the Commission for Energy.

The report contains a long and complex discussion of oil prices, strikingly similar to that produced the previous year by the United Nations Economic Commission for Europe;[6] it deliberately avoided any precise forecast of future prices, but argued that it was possible to identify upper and lower limits. The report suggests that exports of coal from the United States could, in view of the immense resource base, be considered as the marginal source of Europe's energy supply and concluded, therefore, that the price of fuel oil in Europe was unlikely to exceed over any extended period the price of United States' coal adjusted for thermal equivalence, efficiency and convenience. Going in the other direction, the report argued that the price of fuel oil was unlikely to fall below a parity price of domestic European coal, from which it followed that within the period covered by the report (up to 1975) indigenous coal would remain Europe's major source of energy supply.

The Committee analysed all the possible obstacles to the rapid increase in oil supply foreseen by themselves and the Energy Commission; it dismissed the notion that such a spectacular increase was unsustainable, and it concluded that the continued increase in imports and shift of oil refining centres to Europe, which it predicted would happen over the next 20 years, would eventually appear a logical development of the remarkable changes which took place between 1945 and 1955. Analysing the consequences of these developments, the Committee emphasized that the strategic dependence on the Middle East oil producing countries and transit countries was linked inextricably to the unimpeded exchange of resources with Europe, and that mutual dependence would ensure stability. This was a remarkable statement of the doctrine of mutual interdependence which still prevails in the EEC Commission, little elaborated and little advanced.

Partly, no doubt, to counter the dampening effect of the Hartley report, partly to fill the interval between the preparation of the final report of the *Relance* Committee and the beginning of Euratom, partly to encourage ratification of the Euratom Treaty by the French National Assembly, and partly as a simple piece of proselytism, Monnet's Action Committee proposed that a report be prepared to present the case for nuclear energy and to set out the mission of Euratom. Accordingly, in November 1956 the Ministers of Foreign Affairs of the ECSC countries requested Louis Armand, Franceso Giordani (chairman of the Italian Committee for Nuclear Research) and Franz Etzel (a vice-president of the ECSC) to report on the 'amount of atomic energy which can be produced in the near future in the six countries, and the means to be employed for this purpose'. The authors replied in *Target for Euratom*, a document that should be preserved for ever as a dreadful warning of the dangers of expert enthusiasm even from the most distinguished and reputable sources. The preface to *Target for Euratom*[16] asserts that 'today, it can be said, that if our countries, guided and stimulated by Euratom, make the necessary effort they will in future command – as the New World does now – abundant and cheap energy supplies, enabling them to enter boldly into the atomic era'. In the body of the report the authors analyse the consequences for the balance of payments of a dependence on imported oil and make much of the insecurity of supply that the Suez crisis had made so clear; a future stoppage, the authors argue, could be calamitous, and only nuclear energy could protect the European economy; yet nuclear energy was not quite economic. The dilemma was to formulate a 'coefficient of security', that is to say, to decide what extra cost would be tolerated in return for security of supply. The authors advocated a target of 15 GW(e) of installed nuclear capacity in Euratom countries by 1967 – this was considered a practical maximum, the limiting factor being the demand for base load power generation, nuclear energy not yet being thought commercial in any other context. It was proposed that after 1967 construction of nuclear power stations should be planned to ensure that imports of fuel would not increase. Eventually, in 1970, the rate of construction should level out to about 4 GW(e) a year, giving a total nuclear electricity generating capacity in 1975 of about 50 GW(e). The report concedes that this recommendation could not be justified by economics alone, but is based partly on political advantages of security. The proposal received great appreciation from enthusiastic Europeans; one example among many is the *évocation* by Henri Rieben[19] who wrote: 'Key to the future for every European, Euratom is capable of making Europe, at the hour of its greatest decline, the true continent of the future'.

A conjunction of events and skilful management contributed to the acclaim. The Suez canal was closed, there appeared to be an acute threat to Europe's economy, the United Kingdom had responded by tripling its nuclear targets, the reputation of the authors of the *Target* was high, and the whole business, including the pilgrimages to London and Washington that had earned the authors the unofficial title of 'the Three Wise Men', had been widely publicized. But most important of all, the enthusiastic commendation of the U.S.A. had given the report great authority. A joint communiqué of the Three Wise Men and the State Department in Washington declared firstly that the U.S.A. considered that the ambitious programme could be realized, secondly that the U.S.A. would assure Euratom a supply of materials, in particular the essential nuclear fuel, and thirdly that there would follow 'fruitful exchanges' and an 'active association' in pursuit of peaceful uses of atomic energy.[20] In Europe this had the appealing sound of an association of equals, but the motives of the State Department were not altruistic. At the time the role of Euratom was still contentious and it was not clear what contribution the Atomic Energy Community might make to European military endeavours. American enthusiasm for the enormous programme of peaceful uses and its offer (or bait) of enriched uranium were intended to mould Euratom into an organization for producing electricity and to leave it no resources to devote to military affairs. The U.S.A. was at that time, as indeed it still is, reluctant to see more countries acquire the capability of manufacturing nuclear weapons; it had even refused the United Kingdom access to the results of the Manhattan project to which the United Kingdom had contributed its seminal work on the enrichment of uranium. In this matter the interests of the U.S.A. coincided with those of M. Monnet, who saw Euratom as helping to stop the spread of nuclear weapons.

The major literary product of the post-Suez analysis made by the oil camp was the report, again by the Oil Committee of the OEEC, on the implications and lessons of the crisis.[21] This report is mostly given over to an account of measures taken during the crisis and an examination of their success in modifying the economic repercussions. Much of this is no longer of great interest, but the conclusions induce a remarkable sense of *déjà vu* in anyone familiar with recent priorities of energy policy in the EEC. The Committee proposed a variety of measures to minimize the effects of a possible interruption in the supplies of oil to Europe; they were essentially:

(a) to assure the equitable distribution of available supplies between member countries in the event of any future emergency;

(b) to accumulate larger reserves of oil in Europe than had been held up to that time;

(c) to diversify the origin of supplies;

(d) mutual consultation and appropriate planning by government and industry to place Europe in a better position to overcome interruptions.

These recommendations, together with the doctrine of mutual interdependence of Europe and the Middle East described by the same Committee in the earlier report, are still essential elements of Community energy policy.

The lack of concern with hydrocarbons in the *Relance* Committee is surprising when compared with the analysis of the UNECE[6] and the OEEC.[17,18,21] For convenience, the predictions made for 1975 by the Energy Commission of the OEEC and the authors of *Target for Euratom* are compared with the actual consumption in the ECSC countries in 1973.

Fuel Consumption
(million tonnes coal equivalent)

	OEEC[22] (1975)	Target for[23] Euratom (1975)	Actual in ECSC[24] countries (1973)
Indigenous fuel	780	449	371
Hard coal (total)	520	293	} 194
Brown coal	35	49	
Petroleum	50	29	17
Natural gas	25	22	124
Hydroelectric/Geothermal	130	56	36
Nuclear	80	125	10
Imported coal	50	} 157	} 626
Imported petroleum	250–450		
TOTAL	1,160–1,360	731	1,007

The figures for the 17 OEEC countries, including the United Kingdom, obviously are not comparable to predicted or actual figures for the ECSC countries except in the broadest matters of principle; the authors of *Target for Euratom* did compare their own estimates with the OEEC work and concluded that as far as they could tell, given the different scope, the OEEC were slightly less optimistic about indigenous coal production and much less optimistic about nuclear energy. Both groups overestimated the future demands for coal and nuclear energy, and underestimated the future demand for oil, but the OEEC work is consistently more accurate. What is much more important is that the OEEC work correctly predicts the direction, approximate rate of change and principal features of future importance in each sector; this is, in all conscience, the most that one can expect of such a forecast. It should permit appropriate institutions to be established to anticipate the type of change and its general nature; fine tuning is subsequently possible, but the inertia of an inappropriate institutional structure is most inhibiting.

Not only was the future importance of oil clearly recognized within the OEEC, but the main political consequences and proposals to resist them had been thrashed out within the Oil Committee and published by September 1956. The complete absence of any specific reference to these problems in the report of the Commission of experts on conventional energy in the *Relance* Committee is astonishing.

When going over the relative arguments for oil and nuclear energy put forward at that time, it is difficult not to conclude that oil comes off best. *The Price of Oil in Western Europe*[6] had argued convincingly that the price of oil from the Middle East was way above cost and that there

23

were enormous reserves of this low-cost oil available. It was also widely conceded that, even in the prevailing economic circumstances, nuclear energy was not quite commercial but required protection on political grounds. The evidence was therefore available to show that the competitive position of nuclear energy would deteriorate in the future.

With the best will in the world it is difficult to avoid the conclusion that discussion of these matters, which had already been so comprehensively debated in the OEEC, was avoided in the report of the *Relance* Committee in order to avoid detracting from the future importance of nuclear energy and Euratom, and therefore spoiling the opportunity to promote political unity by leading Europe into a new age. This gives the impression that the nuclear vision was really visible to no one, but the reality is more complicated than that. It is valuable to examine why the politicians of the ECSC countries agreed to establish Euratom; one cannot believe that they all consented to appear to share an interpretation of the commercial future for nuclear energy that was contradicted by the known facts.

The group that most consistently and most vigorously supported Euratom was M. Monnet's Action Committee for a United States of Europe. The formation of this Committee was announced in October 1955 during the period in which the *Relance* Committee was preparing its report. Thirty-three leaders of political parties and trade unions in the six member states of the ECSC accepted the invitation to join the Action Committee and undertook by their acceptance to make every effort to secure the support of their organization for M. Monnet's programme of European integration. The list of members is impressive;[25] it includes many of the most powerful political actors of the day. Herr Kurt-Georg Kiesinger (chairman of the Bundestag Foreign Affairs Committee) and Herr Erich Ollenhauer (chairman of the German Social Democratic Party) represented the principal German parties; M. Guy Mollet and M. Maurice Faure were among the French members. The support of this committee for an agency dedicated to peaceful uses of nuclear energy was never veiled. In January 1956 the committee adopted a resolution declaring the Euratom project essential and recommending extensive delegation of authority in this field to a supranational executive.

The most striking aspect of the declaration is the opening: 'To ensure the exclusively peaceful development of atomic energy . . .'; in the eyes of M. Monnet and his Action Committee, Euratom was to be a means of ensuring that Europe remained free of nuclear weapons. In March 1956 this resolution was debated by the Bundestag and adopted, providing as clear a demonstration as any of the striking divergence between France and Germany on the subject of thermonuclear weapons. The overwhelming French desire for 'la bombe' was to be an important influence in the existence and purpose of Euratom.

The government of M. Mollet in France was wholehoartodly Euro
pean. In his investiture speech M. Mollet had proposed that Europe
confine itself to the peaceful use of atomic weapons, but there was never
any chance of that attitude being widely shared in France. The majority
of French politicians were obsessed by the idea that France must develop her own nuclear weapons.[26] The draft provisions of the Euratom
treaty had envisaged that the members of the Atomic Community
would undertake not to test nuclear weapons within the first five years,
and that at the end of the transitional period the Community would
decide on a majority vote whether to restore to its members the freedom
to make and test nuclear devices. This was quite unacceptable to various
members of the French Cabinet and, in order to keep his government
together, M. Mollet was forced to concede that he would insist on the
provisions of the Treaty being amended so that at the end of the transitional period all members, with the exception of Germany, would
automatically regain their right to test atomic weapons. The matter
was debated by the French National Assembly on 11 July 1956.

Before the debate the Assembly heard, at the request of M. Mollet,
statements from the two leading nuclear technocrats of the time,
M. Francis Perrin (High Commissioner for Atomic Energy) and
M. Louis Armand. Both spoke of the peaceful uses of atomic energy
and both explained that the costs of the enterprise exceeded the resources of France alone and that European collaboration was essential
if the increasing deficiency of energy supplies to the continent was to
be made up by nuclear energy. But the members of the Assembly were
more concerned about the effect Euratom might have on the national
policy for the defence of France; they were determined that Euratom
should not impede the development of a French atomic bomb. The
Minister of National Defence assured the Assembly that Euratom
would help, not hinder, France in preparing her own weapons, because
it would enable a more economical deployment of resources in basic
nuclear technology. M. Mollet, in winding up the debate, eloquently
expounded the dominant political objective of the whole manoeuvre,
that Germany should be integrated into Europe and prevented from
turning to the East by weaving between her and France numerous
economic, political and cultural links. A resolution in favour of the
negotiations was adopted, but the mood of the National Assembly
signalled to the other member states (as it was intended to do) that if
they went ahead with Euratom in its present form, then it would go
the same way as the European Defence Community, one of the most
unacceptable provisions of which, from the French point of view,
would have been to limit their nuclear weapons programme.

To understand how the French could be so enthusiastic for Euratom
when they regarded it as a potential threat, one must understand how

25

weak France was in nuclear matters; her access to fuel was poor, her industrial base was much weaker than Germany's, and her technical knowledge was indifferent. The specific French technical expectations from Euratom were:[10,26,27]

(a) to obtain technical information; this idea could be reasonably entertained because it was proposed that Euratom should remain open to the participation or association of other OEEC countries; the French made much of the desirability of luring the United Kingdom into Euratom or into co-operation with Euratom;

(b) to obtain access to fuel; although France has deposits of uranium they are not easily workable; Belgium controlled rich uranium deposits in the Congo which, within a common market, would be accessible to France;

(c) Germany would supply finance, an industrial base, nuclear technology and the chemical expertise required for reprocessing irradiated fuel elements to obtain plutonium for weapons; France also considered it essential to prevent Germany from developing its own nuclear industry, either independently or in co-operation with the U.S.A.; during the debate in the National Assembly members suggested that Germany wanted to see Euratom fail so that she could be independently pre-eminent in the field; this was certainly true of some German industrialists.

The extent to which membership of Euratom would prevent or assist France in becoming a nuclear power was the crucial question underlying the negotiations on Euratom; there was plenty of scope for manoeuvre because there was no natural reason why Euratom should not either assist or prevent member states from individual military ventures; all depended on the design of the institution. The ambiguity of the military and commercial functions of nuclear energy showed through particularly in three topics which dominated the final negotiations for Euratom. They were:

(a) what priority should be given to the construction by Euratom of a plant for separating isotopes of uranium;

(b) whether the membership of Euratom would restrict the testing and development of nuclear weapons;

(c) the military significance of the proposal that Euratom should have a monopoly of fissile materials.

The report of the *Relance* Committee had proposed that the construction of a gaseous diffusion plant for separating isotopes of uranium should have high priority. In this France and Germany were in broad agreement. The venture was predicated on the grounds that the plant would alleviate the strategic dependence on imported nuclear fuel, but it would also have given European countries the opportunity to build weapons at a later date. At first, France was strongly committed to the project because she thought it beyond her own resources. The U.S.A. was strongly opposed, and therefore endorsed the massive commercial programme and offered to supply the enriched uranium that would be needed. Consequently, when M. Armand returned from Washington he no longer thought enrichment plant should be so high in European priorities. By this time France had convinced herself that she had the resources to build her own plant, which for military affairs was much more convenient; she therefore did not then oppose the shift in priorities.

The proposal that the Community should have monopoly ownership of nuclear materials and supplies had interesting ambiguities for French military ambitions. If Euratom members were commited to peaceful uses, the Community monopoly rights to fuel and materials would reinforce that obligation and inhibit independent ventures. If, on the other hand, it was clearly understood that the Atomic Community would not stop national military ventures, then the monopoly right could help such ventures. It was for this reason that France fought hard for the Community monopoly.

Some opinion in Germany, despite the adoption by the Bundestag of the Action Committee's resolution, was opposed to the Community monopoly, both on free-market principles and on the grounds that the French were seeking control over still more strategic German industry through a common institution, as they had done through the ECSC. This opinion was particularly prevalent in the German chemical industry.

The outstanding matters were finally settled in February 1957; the French obtained everything they wanted. Euratom was to have exclusive ownership of special fissionable materials whether produced in or imported into the Community, thus giving France access to supplies, but materials intended for national defence were not owned by Euratom, thus preserving for France the plutonium from her military reactors, both operating and planned. Euratom had responsibility for control of all nuclear fuel other than that produced for defence. France also obtained explicit recognition of her right to explode atomic bombs. Finally she obtained a concession that the sharing of nuclear information in the Community should be restricted if a member state's defence interests were affected; the concession benefited France alone.

The conjunction of motives that led to the formation of Euratom can be summarized as follows. France wanted Euratom partly because some of her politicians believed it to be a significant help in European integration, but mainly because she thought it would expedite her weapons programme. French politicians were generally much less enthusiastic about the Common Market than they were about Euratom, and proponents of Euratom in France were careful to make it clear that they considered the ventures as being quite separate; commitment to one did not imply commitment to the other. But the five other member states favoured the Common Market and were in varying degrees unenthusiastic about Euratom. Although it would be an exaggeration to say Euratom was conceded to the French in exchange for the Common Market, it is probably true that Euratom would not have been formed without the intensive French backing. The 'Europeans', represented by M. Monnet's Action Committee, had as their principal political objective the unification of Europe; for them nuclear energy appeared the perfect case of an expanding economic sector in rapid change developed in common, helping to create an economic and technical interdependence that would prevent conflict and induce political integration. The motive of this Committee was exclusively political. Indeed, the conjunction of motives leading to Euratom were all political; the *initiative* was never a perception that nuclear energy as an economic sector required or justified a Community institution; when the political motives required technical support, they fell back on a technical vision of the future which was an extreme view that did not enjoy the best of the arguments even at the time.

The most suitable event to choose to close the discussion of this period of history is the agreement, by the Council of Ministers of the ECSC, of a Protocol for an energy policy.[28] The Protocol had been preceded by another visionary report in the heavy contemporary crop.[29] This one comprised a comprehensive review of energy flows within the six; it appeared between the Hartley report and the *Target for Euratom* and served as the statistical basis for the latter work. It was produced by the 'Mixed Committee', comprising members from the High Authority and the Council of Ministers; this committee had been set up in 1953 to inquire into all aspects of the energy situation, so that the High Authority would have the information necessary to formulate objectives for the coal and steel industries. The report was the first sound statistical record of energy flows in the six; it clearly showed the decrease in the proportion of energy consumption being met by indigenous sources, declining from 82 per cent in 1950 to 70 per cent in 1955. The authors were in large part those responsible for the chapter on conventional energy in the report of the *Relance* Committee, so the report is also interesting as a more detailed exposition of their thinking. As a consequence of the report, the High Authority and the Council of Ministers adopted in October 1957 the Protocol for an energy policy. The Protocol showed no development of thought but essentially tied up the procedural ends left over from the *Relance* Committee and charged the High Authority, by means of the Mixed Committee, with keeping an eye on what was happening in the rest of the energy market.

Its symbolic significance is that it was the first step on the long and painful road to a common energy policy, the end of which is not yet in sight.[30]

C. A Time of Perseverance

... deciding what the price of energy in Europe should be involved two equally serious risks:
—prices might be set too low, thus jeopardizing political stability and thereby the future price of energy;
—prices might be set too high, thus hindering industrial expansion and the Community's export capacity.

The High Authority continued to believe that there could be no abandonment of the essential aim of energy policy, which was ultimately to make this crucial choice in common.

The High Authority of the ECSC,[31] 1964.

1. COAL POLICY

The early days of the new Communities, up to about 1963, are generally thought of as a Golden Age; they are remembered as a period of innovation, simple procedure and tangible results. This recollection may be accurate in some sectors, but it is far from true of energy. The ECSC was to experience its period of greatest difficulty and its supranational authority was to receive a shock from which it has never recovered. Euratom was to have difficulty in getting off the ground. The initiative in energy policy was to come almost exclusively from outside the Community Executive.

In 1956 the High Authority had been planning further increases in coal-mining capacity. On the basis of the usual arguments about the insecurity of oil supplies and the estimated rate of development of nuclear energy, the High Authority recommended an increase in European coal production of 30 million tons per annum by 1975, to give a total production of 320 million tons per annum. Some areas were incapable of producing more, but it was expected that these would maintain production and that the increase would come from the Ruhr, Saar, Lorraine, Campine and Aachen. The Ruhr was to account for 20 million tons of the increase.

There was in the General Report for that year[32] no presentiment of catastrophe, and there was no discussion of the contemporary arguments that the price of oil might decline;[6] it was confidently asserted that there were plentiful markets for economically minable coal.

In 1958/59 industrial activity slackened, the winters were mild; the consumption of energy fell for the first time since the war, but the volume of coal and oil imports continued to increase. More oil was imported because the difference in price, after allowing for convenience

29

and efficiency, justified reinvestment in oil-burning equipment even in the recession. More coal was imported because, in the preceding years of shortage, long-term contracts had been concluded to buy foreign coal; it was especially aggravating that the price in the long term contracts was, not surprisingly, higher than the price of imported coal prevailing during the recession. The result of all this was that the effect of the slight fall in total energy consumption was amplified many times on the indigenous coal industry. From 1957 to 1958 stocks of coal at the pithead in ECSC countries rose from 7.3 million tons to 24.7 million tons, despite a fall in production, and they rose further the following year to 31.2 million tons.

It was impossible not to recognize that this was the result of permanent changes in the structure of energy supply and that these changes and their consequences were by no means over. The oil companies' policy of situating oil refineries ever nearer the final market was well advanced. At first the refineries were built at points on the European coastline where oil could conveniently be imported; subsequently they were built near the great industrial regions and supplied from the coast by pipeline. Technical improvements in shipping also lowered costs. Commercial forces contributed to bring oil prices down. The cartel among the major oil companies, the seven sisters, was challenged by new companies which sought to penetrate the market by offering lower prices; the most flamboyant of these, if not the most successful, was the *Ente Nazionale Idrocarburi* (ENI) vitalized by Enrico Mattei. At the same time the oil producing governments pressed the oil companies to produce more because they saw this as a means of increasing their revenues. A protectionist policy in the U.S.A. forced oil into Europe and, finally, the U.S.S.R. monopoly organization for exports – *Soyuznetexport* – began selling again on the world markets at below current prices. Soviet oil had been sold in Europe before, in the 1920s, but sales abroad had stopped when home demand for oil outgrew supply. Now that prolific fields had been developed in the U.S.S.R. exports began again. The oil was sold vigorously, as it was one of the few commodities in which the U.S.S.R. could compete with the West for quality. The inevitable result of all these forces and of the considerable gap that existed between the cost and the price of Middle East oil was to bring down the general level of prices.

These changes in the energy market coincided with important political changes. The principal parties in the coalition governing France at the time the new Communities were created had been committed to European integration, especially the French Socialist Party. But now a new wave of French nationalism brought General de Gaulle to power. In Germany latent resentment against those provisions of the Treaty of Paris that had been designed to prevent German firms from dominating the coal and steel industries, combined with the unfavourable situation of those industries, led the government to oppose the High Authority. The revival of nationalism and the poor fortunes of the coal industry reinforced each other and put great strain on the ECSC.

The reaction of each member state to the change in available energy supplies differed according to its conception of its own interests. The interest of different member states was determined by a balance of several factors: their commitment to the past, the reading of the future, their desire for low prices and the extent of their adherence to free-market principles. The commitment to the past comprises not only existing capital investment in equipment for mining and using coal, but also the existing investment of people's lives. The skills of mining are not easily acquired and not easily brought together on the same spot to mine coal; they are therefore not reproducible; to destroy them means a concomitant surrender of ability to mine coal in the future. Moreover, because coal mining skills are not of much use in other industry, and because the people possessing them are concentrated in areas where there often may not be other employment, there is some reason to keep on mining coal even if, superficially, it is not profitable. Three reasons can be identified: the labour, if not mining coal, would not be productive at all; the people having committed their lives to an unfortunate industry deserve support; there is always a risk of violent social disruption in coal-mining areas if the industry should fail, and this was taken seriously at the time.

Associated with the extent of the commitment to the past is the reading of the future. If the coal industry were expected to revive at a later date then it would be reasonable to protect it from costly changes not in line with long-term trends. The measures for protection that would be most appropriate would also vary depending on whether it was intended to preserve the industry for future requirements, or to ease its decline.

Low energy prices are attractive to all countries because they strengthen the manufacturing industries and contribute directly to a high standard of living. Conflict only arises if there is also a commitment to the past, or if prices are expected to rise in the future and it is necessary to anticipate the consequences. The latter feature was of no concern in the 1950s, although it is now.

The extent of philosophical commitment to free-market principles influenced the reaction of member states to the crisis in so far as it influenced the nature of the protection preferred and the extent of the struggle with their consciences, which means the extent of the struggle with dominant groups in their political constituency.

Germany was the bastion of free-market principles; it had resolutely supported the High Authority in its actions to abolish cartels and introduce a common market in coal and coal products; it had even gone further and abolished a turnover tax on heavy fuel oil. Its reaction to the crisis, however, was determined by its need to protect and conciliate its home coal industry. The government refused licences for new import contracts, tried to commute existing long-term contracts, imposed a temporary duty on imports in excess of a 5 million ton quota, authorized an emergency selling cartel and reimposed the turnover tax on heavy fuel oil.

Belgium also had free-market principles, but its coal was high-cost and it introduced protectionist measures, including restrictions on imports from third countries, even earlier than Germany. Many Belgian coal miners were nevertheless put on short-time working and there was continual violence in the mining areas.

The French economy was directed by central planning, three principal energy industries were nationalized (*Gaz de France, Electricité de France, Charbonnages de France*), and the oil industry was controlled; the number of oil importers was restricted; investment in oil required prior authorization, and the state helped finance oil prospecting in the Sahara. During the crisis France limited imports of coal from third countries, but the balance of her interest between protection and low prices lay more towards low prices than it did for Germany and Belgium. The coal industry in France, although substantial, was never as important a political force as in Germany and Belgium; France was to be seduced more rapidly than Germany by the benefits of cheap oil.

Italy had no indigenous energy production to speak of and a deep-seated conviction that its recurring economic problems were largely a result of that deficiency; the recent *miracolo italiano* was beginning to fade and Italian opinion was in favour of buying the cheapest available fuel, including Soviet oil. As Enrico Mattei remarked with acerbity, he could not remember that the coal mining countries of north-west Europe, who were rich when Italy was poor, had at the time offered to share their wealth with his compatriots.[33] The Italian oil market was regulated by maximum prices for consumer sales, there was a national oil company, and investment in the oil industry required authorization. The Netherlands subscribed in principle to a free market, but sought in practice to restrict coal imports to protect their industries.

The High Authority tried at first to deal with the crisis as if it were an ephemeral affair by endeavouring to interpret the rules of the common market as leniently as was possible without infringing the Treaty. Prices of imported coal had fallen from a level about 50 per cent or more above European prices to a level a little below; there was a danger of an all-out price war in Europe. This the High Authority tried to avoid by conceding a limited and controlled war; it authorized limited rebates and price cuts and attempted to stabilize sales and control imports. It got little help from the Council.

In April 1958 the High Authority approached the Council, asking it to permit arrangements whereby the Community would finance the stockpiling of saleable coal produced in excess of demand. There was not unanimous agreement. It asked again in October, and after lengthy negotiation a temporary·system was agreed. During this time the member states were resorting increasingly to national initiatives. In February 1958 Belgium restricted imports from third countries and in September 1958 Germany did likewise. For these countries the High Authority was obliged to concede that imports of coal be inspected to check that they were from other Community countries.

The High Authority concluded that it was justified in declaring a state of manifest crisis in the coal sector and thereby invoking its powers of Community intervention; it proposed to introduce production quotas and restrict imports. The declaration required to be endorsed by the Council, but only on a majority vote.

The High Authoirty first put this to the Council in March 1959, but had difficulty in defining acceptable proposals.[34] The request was discussed again in May 1959 and again the Council withheld its consent; the High Authority insisted on a vote; France, Germany and Italy opposed the request, the Benelux countries supported it.

The decision was a great blow to the authority of the executive and to future prospects of supranationalism; the resistance of France and Germany had been inspired less by a belief that the measures proposed were inappropriate than by a reluctance to permit interference with what they now saw as their sovereign affairs. The French minister argued that he could not agree to a scheme which would give powers to the High Authority that would affect national industries and have economic, social and political consequences that would devolve on national governments. Thereafter the High Authority was forced to accept that in practice it could exercise the supranational powers conferred on it by the Treaty only with the consent of the member states.[2]

As the economic recession came to an end the demand for energy strengthened; the problems in the coal sector were relieved, but in essence remained. The High Authority was faced with a wide variety of measures taken at a national level to meet the situation in particular countries and not in the Community as a whole; these measures comprised various taxes and duties on heavy oil and various restrictions on imports of coal. The Executive had lost much of its authority and, more seriously, it had lost the prestige, unjustified but real, of presiding over the distribution of an expanding resource.

The High Authority recognized at this stage that demand for coal would not recover in the foreseeable future; it identified the pressing need for a co-ordinated energy policy that would ease the process of adjusting Community coal industries to the new situation in a way that would avoid social disruption, and it set out to devise such a policy within the Inter-Executive Working Party on Energy. To open up the discussion the Working Party produced in March 1960 an interim memorandum setting out the options;[35] it proposed as objectives of an energy policy, low cost, a common market, security, and a dependable minimum volume of supplies; it recognized that these objectives conflicted and that priorities had to be established. To compare these objectives required a common measure and in a free-market system the proper measure is price. The Inter-Executive Working Party therefore concluded from this analysis that the essential decision was to determine a price for energy that would serve as a guide to all. The guide price was not specified, but the considerations affecting the decision were clearly stated. If the aim were to devise a low-cost energy policy that would benefit manufacturing industries and other consumers then the guide price should be set at about the level of the expected price of imported energy; if the aim were to allow a margin of preference for Community fuels then the guide price should be set higher, in which case other protective devices would be needed to prevent excessive imports. If so desired a high guidance price could be progressively reduced, thus eventually offering the benefits of low-cost energy to the Community, but making the transition with minimum social dislocation.

This analysis does not really exhaust the possibilities; it asserts that the guidance price would define the amount of Community production capacity that would remain in being. But this is not so, it depends also on the extent of subsidy; the Executive eschewed subsidies in their analysis because subsidies were explicitly forbidden by the Treaty of Paris, but it would have been technically possible to have a low-price energy policy with high Community production aided by massive subsidies. The really crucial question was how much Community production capacity should be kept in being; an answer to that question would define the costs to be borne by the Community; the next step would be to decide how those costs were to be allocated, for example who was to provide the money and to what extent Community production capacity should be protected by subsidy and to what extent by import restrictions; a different balance of those two factors would redistribute the burden. Subsidies, therefore, make the policy more flexible and facilitate balancing the interests of the consuming and producing countries.

As it was, in terms of the analysis in the interim memorandum, there was no way of balancing the interest of France and Italy in low-cost energy and the interest of Germany and others in maintaining their coal mining industries. After various abortive studies and further exhortation from the European Parliament, in April 1962 the Council of Ministers directed the three Executives to submit joint proposals for a common policy, specifying that the Executives need not confine themselves to the legal possibilities of the existing Treaties. This provision was probably meant to authorize subsidies. In June 1962 the Executives submitted to the Council another memorandum suggesting what would now be called a policy U-turn.[36,37] The memorandum proposed a low-price energy policy; all fuels except from the Soviet bloc would be allowed unimpeded into the country, thereby permitting the Community to benefit in manufacturing and trade. The world price for oil would automatically set the price at which other fuels would compete, after allowance for heat content, efficiency and convenience. The authors of the memorandum expected that, with what they considered the most likely assumptions about the price of American coal and imported oil, only about 50 per cent of the 1961 coal production would be competitive by 1970; they also recognized that for social reasons and for reasons of security Community coal production should be assisted; the assistance should be provided both by subsidy and protection in order to spread the burden; they insisted, however, that the Community should take this decision in common. Subsidies would be removed in three stages, the last beginning in 1970. The memorandum envisaged no substantial role for nuclear power in the next ten years.

In many ways this was a sensible document which recognized the benefits of a low-cost energy policy and sought to find a consensus on the extent to which indigenous production should be protected; it was analytically consistent and its proposals were a logical consequence of the analysis. It was not, however, well received.

The reason for this was partly the conflicting interests of the member states, but there also seems to have been dissension among the three Commissions. Although there was intellectual agreement that low cost and security were incompatible, the priority to be given to these objectives was a matter of contention. It is interesting to compare the contemporary publications of the three Communities[38-43] with the memorandum itself. The EEC put great weight on low cost, and believed that nuclear power should be required to prove itself commercially and did not merit protection. The ECSC laid great stress on the security of indigenous coal, but took a similar line on nuclear power. Euratom stressed the need to keep the long-term in mind, implying that to facilitate and anticipate the development of nuclear energy in the future it should be given some preference in the present. The power in the energy sector lay with the ECSC, the EEC coming second and Euratom a poor third. The divided responsibility for energy did not show up as

35

an unhappy compromise in the joint proposals, but may have impeded their prosecution.

The policy set out in the memorandum was eventually cast into concrete proposals, amended and modified to accommodate some of the vested interests of member states, but it was difficult to obtain agreement despite the efforts of the executive. Finally, in December 1963, the Council rejected the draft agreement on the conditions for a common market in energy submitted to them by the Commission. An alternative draft was submitted by Germany, but the High Authority, in a thundering declaration reminiscent of better times in the European movement, rejected it as 'wholly inadequate' and castigated the governments of the coal-producing countries for introducing measures that were 'more and more exclusively national'.

Then, in the truly best style of the European Executive, members of the Working Party set out for the capitals of the member states preaching the doctrine and raising support. In this they were successful and a Protocol of Agreement on energy policy was finally adopted by a special Council of Ministers of the ECSC on 21 April 1964.[44]

This Protocol occupies an important place in the lore of the common energy policy. It was hailed as the first decisive agreement since the Community set out to create a common policy in 1957 and was compared to the progress achieved in the common agricultural policy.[45] The enthusiasm was a little exaggerated but it is easy to understand the relief of the High Authority. The general principles agreed were similar to those of the 1957 Protocol, but the new agreement was important in three ways. Firstly as a symbol of solidarity after a period of rampant nationalism, secondly in the practical measures now permitted to the Community Executive to deal with the crisis in the coal industry, and thirdly in that the Community had finally accepted the need to subsidize indigenous production, thereby permitting it to remain in being at a relatively low overall price for energy.

It is unlikely that the Community could have agreed on anything but a low-price policy; the reasons for adopting a high-price policy could only be for the security of indigenous supply and to avoid social costs, but these are only compelling reasons for the producing country; consuming countries would not bear the social costs in any case and, because of the difficulty of reorganizing established trading patterns rapidly in times of crisis, it is unlikely that they would ever benefit from the security of supply. The producing country has nothing to offer the consuming country in exchange for a high-price policy; no resource is created by the high price to the benefit of both parties. Specifically Italy, and to a slightly lesser extent France, would not have contributed to Community financing of aids to German coal mines when they would not have benefited from the security of supply. This point is worth making in detail because similar considerations still prevail today and are sometimes not clearly recognized.

But, going back to 1964, the High Authority was charged as a matter of urgency to implement a co-ordinated system of state aids or subsidies; it duly prepared proposals that member states would notify the High Authority of intended subsidies, and the Authority would authorize them if they fulfilled certain criteria adopted by the Community, essentially if they were not thought to disturb competition between mines.

This procedure was known as a Community system of state aids; the money came from the country in which the subsidized coal field existed and was disbursed by the government of that country, but the act was authorized by the High Authority according to Community criteria. Operating the system did give the High Authority the incidental benefit of obtaining for the first time complete information on the assistance being given to collieries. There was no element of Community finance; essentially the system was a recognition of what was already happening, but by agreeing on common rules it was given the air of a common policy. The measures were to apply until 1967.

Although some order had been brought to the various national attempts to protect coal, the basic problem remained. The price of petroleum products in the Community was falling, coal prices were stable; pithead stocks of coal were rising even though production was falling. The next step was to agree how much Community capacity was to be kept in production. Evidently, as there was no Community element in the finance of subsidies for coal, it was unlikely that the coal-producing countries would be enthusiastic about any proposal for the Community to influence the decision on what quantity of coal producing capacity should be protected. However, optimism being the prerequisite quality for a Community official, in March 1966 the High Authority prepared an opinion on the future of the coal industry.[46]

This memorandum proposed that the Community's best course was to accept a target of 190 million tons by 1970; this would permit indigenous sources to supply about 50 per cent of the predicted consumption of energy. The target was 30 million tons less than the output in 1965, but was still 15 million tons more than the amount of coal the High Authority thought would be competitive if no support were given. The High Authority did not propose to guarantee sales of 190 million tons, but thought that either duties, quotas, tax devices or subsidies for steam coal should be introduced to give a good chance of achieving that target. It was considered self-evident that subsidy was the correct form of protection for coking coal, because the steel industry had to compete in world markets and therefore required cheap energy.

The reluctance to guarantee sales is an aspect of another thorny theme that has run through Community energy policy. The uncertain future of the coal industry has been put forward continuously since about 1958 as a reason for requiring governments to provide some measure of guarantee for future sales; without this support, it is argued, the necessary investment in new mines will not be made. On the other hand a formal guarantee of sales would weaken the incentive to keep wages down and productivity up; formal guarantees have not been given even by the government in the United Kingdom, where the political influence of the mining unions is strong and where the industry is nationalized and presumably intended to escape to some extent the discipline of market forces. Guaranteed sales would have offended much more strongly the principles of competition on which the Communities were constructed.

Protection without guaranteed sales evidently does not give the same confidence in the future of the industry, but it is as much as could be expected in the Community. The memorandum was in any case to come to grief even in its modest undertaking.

The significance of the memorandum is that the High Authority proposed measures whereby the Community, acting as one, would protect indigenous coal production. It was submitted first to the Coal Problems Committee, an *ad hoc* committee of senior government officials, chaired by the High Authority, but they could agree neither on the extent nor the nature of protection. The coal producing countries, especially Germany, pushed for Community protection both indirectly through import quotas and duties and directly through Community financial aids. The energy importing countries objected, especially Italy and France and to a lesser extent the Netherlands. Germany forced its arguments in the Council and finally requested the High Authority to declare a 'manifest crisis'. The High Authority gave its opinion that the problem afflicting the German coal industry was not temporary, but was a structural contraction and could not be dealt with by Community action. Germany then undertook, at its own expense, without Community aid or guarantees, to reorganize its coal industry. The question of how much Community coal to keep in production and what Community protection to offer sank without trace.

The episode clearly shows the progressive deterioration in the authority and confidence of the Executives. If the Executives were not prepared to support Germany in its claim for Community protection of the coal industry then they should never have undertaken to try to determine what Community capacity should be kept in production. The Executives presumably did not want to go through the trauma of attempting to obtain consent to a declaration of manifest crisis when they knew full well that it might not be granted and that, at the worst, to carry the dispute any further might have harmed, spiritually or materially, the forthcoming merger of the Executives.

With coking coal the High Authority was more successful in its efforts to inject a Community element into the protection of indigenous industry. The reasons for this were simply that France had an interest in protecting its coking coal industry and the consuming countries had a stake in the security of supply through established trading patterns.

The pressure on indigenous production came from American imports; Italy and the Netherlands had built steel works on coastal sites and therefore benefited from the availability of these low-price imports. As a consequence, demand on German collieries fell and, it was argued, competition among steel producers in the Community was distorted. This latter contention is extremely dubious because preferential access to imported raw materials is a perfectly sound basis for the sort of specialization and lower costs that the customs union was expected to provide. However, the argument carried weight at the time.

In July 1966 the Authority proposed a flexible scheme of subsidies calculated on the basis of geographical factors. The principal feature was an element of subsidy from a Community fund financed by contributions from all six governments. The proposal was vigorously supported by the German Government and the German coal and steel industry, but resisted by the Netherlands and Italy and also by the French, who argued that it was premature in the absence of a common energy policy. The French assertion was part of an attempt to get preferential terms for Saharan petroleum products as part of a 'package' of proposals for energy policy. The probability that Germany and France would give independent national support to their industries stimulated the High Authority to another tour of European capitals in search of support for its proposals. The European Parliament gave its usual loyal support by appealing for a European solution to the problem. The proposals were modified several times to suit France and finally adopted at the beginning of 1967. Subsidies for metallurgical coking coal and coke produced and used within a state would be paid by the government of that state. Subsidies for sales to other Community countries would be paid 40 per cent by the producing country and 60 per cent by a common fund, with an upper limit, for each of the two years covered (1967 and 1968), of 22 million units of account. The fund was financed by the six in the proportions: Germany 28 per cent, Belgium 11 per cent, France 28 per cent, Italy 14 per cent, Luxembourg 9 per cent, Netherlands 10 per cent. This agreement was a high point in Community energy policy in that it was the first, and is still the only, significant Community action, albeit that the element of Community subsidy was small.

2. OIL AND NATURAL GAS POLICY

Meanwhile the Commission of the European Economic Community had begun to formulate the principles of a common policy for oil and natural gas, as they had been instructed to do by the Council in the 1964 Protocol of Agreement. The Commission reiterated the arguments of the OEEC and the ECE from several years previously, which had been passed over in the reports of the *Relance* Committee, and identified as their first priority the dangers of relying on a supply of energy that might be interrupted for economic or political reasons.

The Commission proposed, as had the OEEC,[18,21] that European companies should co-operate with other consumers, analyse the possibilities of sharing supplies and stockpile petroleum products. The Commission also advised that exploration in the Community should be promoted and that subsidies for indigenous production of petroleum might be provided. This last idea was associated with the recent heavy investments that had been made in Groningen and Saharan gas. The French were by no means sure how the cost of Saharan gas would compare with world prices and would have appreciated subsidies. The second priority of the Commission was to establish a common market in petroleum products free of any obstruction to trade or disturbance of competition. The Commission thought that some national arrangements for the control of petroleum imports might conflict with the principles of a common market, particularly those pertaining in France, but to a lesser extent also those in Germany and Italy; it proposed freedom of establishment, especially for exploration licences, and a common commercial policy co-ordinating pipeline regulations, rules of sale, and taxes. The Commission did not discuss to what extent fuels should be allowed to compete and to what extent they should be protected; this would have trespassed on High Authority ground. The European Parliament gave almost unqualified support for these proposals, but the Commission did not push them and no doubt intended them as a five-finger exercise to test part of a complete energy policy being prepared for the merger of the Executives.

3. NUCLEAR POLICY

Of the specific objectives of Euratom, three are especially relevant to energy policy: establishment of a nuclear common market, research and development, and procurement of nuclear fuel. Euratom was to establish a common market in nuclear materials and equipment, devise a plan for permitting nuclear workers to move freely, agree conventions for insurance, lay down standards for health protection and in general remove all artificial obstacles to trade. For research and development it was given an initial budget for five years (1958–62) of £75 million, and later twice as much for the following quinquennium (1963–67). Four joint research centres were set up, at Ispra, Petten, Geel and Karlsruhe; the most heavily funded of these was Ispra. The principal project was to develop a European reactor, the costs of which would eventually be recovered in part by sales abroad. The Community effort began with ORGEL, a design for a reactor cooled by an organic liquid and moderated by heavy water. Euratom was also intended to run and partly finance joint enterprises. Among those first thought of were a gaseous diffusion plant and a fuel reprocessing plant. These projects were dropped almost immediately and the concept of joint enterprise was soon downgraded to mean any project on which the Community wished to confer some Community status. Several joint ventures, without Community control, did develop, often with countries outside the Community, especially the U.S.A. Some of this joint work was done on advanced gas-cooled reactors, the technology favoured by the United Kingdom; specific projects were Dragon at Winfrith in the United Kingdom and the Thorium High-Temperature Reactor at Jülich in Germany. Some work was also done on fast reactors, and Euratom put up some of the money for the German nuclear merchant ship, the *Otto Hahn*.

There were also provisions in the Treaty for a joint Supply Agency that would permit the Community to devise a joint policy for the procurement of ores, raw materials and special fissile material on the basis of equal access to available resources. It was intended that the Agency conduct its affairs by commercial standards, subject to control by the Commission. It possessed extensive powers; it had an option to purchase any of the materials in question that were produced by member states and it had an exclusive right to conclude contracts for the purchase or sale of such materials outside the Community. The Agency would endeavour to satisfy all applications for ores, raw materials and special fissile matter, but if unable to do so fully it would fairly distribute what was available, according to a common nuclear policy to be decided.

Euratom also took upon itself an indicative planning function, although it had no powers under the Treaty to give its plans or targets any practical significance; at the most they were exhortatory. The first effort in this respect took place outside the institution and was published as the *Target for Euratom* which aimed at 15 GW(e) by 1967. In the third General Report in 1960 the Commission abandoned that target, acknowledged that development would be slower than previously expected, foresaw less than 10 GW(e) of installed capacity by 1970, but recommended a target of 40 GW(e) by 1980.

In all these four functions – establishment of a nuclear common market, research and development, procurement of nuclear fuel and indicative planning – Euratom more or less failed, for reasons whose nature varied for the different functions.

Euratom has probably done its best work in creating a common market and common standards for nuclear technology, but unfortunately its success even here has been vitiated by its failure in all other functions. Under the Treaty, Euratom was responsible for the security of all nuclear fuel other than that involved in military affairs. Consequently, Euratom was obliged to devise acceptable standards of security and to employ inspectors to check stocks of material and supervise operations. This it did satisfactorily. But designs of reactors, procedures for licensing, standards of safety and quality control have never been harmonized, and as the commercial importance of nuclear power has increased, so the scope and consequences of this divergence have widened.

Broadly, the research and development function of Euratom failed completely. No Community design of reactor was developed; those built for commercial purposes were either from the U.S.A., France or the United Kingdom. There were a number of reasons for this. The Joint Enterprises fell through when France realized she had the resources to go ahead on her own, and when the U.S.A. offered to provide all the enriched uranium necessary for the commercial nuclear power programme in Europe. From the beginning there was little sharing of technological information between the two principal member states. France pursued her own national programme with vigour and exploited the escape clause in the Treaty which suspended the obligation to share information within the Community if the defence interests of a member state were affected. In practice this meant that France had only to state that a research centre had a military nature and all information about the work done there could be classed as secret. German industrialists exhibited an equal lack of Community spirit in a rather different way; from the outset, indeed before Euratom was formed, they had identified their interests as lying in the exploitation of United States' technology under licence, thereby making the most of their industrial base and minimizing the consequences of their weaknesses in fundamental research.

When the expenditure by Euratom passed the limit permitted by the budget in the second quinquennium the member states refused to provide any significant supplement. To make ends meet the French insisted that research on the light-water reactors be cut back and the principal effort be concentrated on fast reactors. The French believed that the fast reactor was the most satisfactory answer to the perennial question of security of supply and also offered Europe the opportunity to leap-frog American technology and escape from the persistent domination of the U.S.A.

Although there was some intrinsic merit in this argument, it was largely perceived by other member states as symptomatic of the general French attitude to Euratom. Although at the outset she had been so insistent about Euratom, France had eventually found she could in practice do more on her own than she had first thought; she therefore treated Euratom partly as a supplement to her own programme and a means of getting advanced research done at Community expense, and partly as a vehicle for imposing her technology on the Community and thereby defraying the costs of her own programme. Adventuring for a moment outside the limits of this period, in October 1968 after the second quinquennium had expired, the Commission submitted a new research programme for the third quinquennium with the principal objectives of developing a fast reactor and constructing an enrichment plant. For a time it appeared that the Council of Ministers might reject the programme almost entirely and cut the research and development work of Euratom to nothing. In the end humanitarian feelings prevailed and the research institutions have been kept ticking over, but essentially they lost all residual significance in 1968. In more recent time there has been some resurgence of a common research effort in nuclear energy, albeit not under the Community aegis, in the form of attempts by France and Germany to agree on co-operation in the development of fast reactors.

The Euratom Supply Agency, with its fearsome array of powers, turned out in practice to be quite docile. Since the formation of Euratom there has been a persistent glut of uranium ore and there has been no advantage in proceeding through a Community purchasing agency. Consequently, the Commission agreed to a procedure whereby it should simply receive retrospective notification of contracts·for the purchase of uranium. This simplified procedure was agreed for a limited period, and the Commission has periodically proposed a return to a more demanding regime. In 1974 it proposed that the Supply Agency be required to give prior approval to contracts entered into by Community producers and users of uranium. The proposal was unpopular with most national delegations and nothing has yet come of it. The Supply Agency has had no significant effect on Community life; this is not to say that the institution has failed, but simply that the need for it has never materialized. If, as one respectable line of argument suggests, there were to be a shortage of uranium in the future and the Supply Agency were to recover its interventionist powers, then it might become an effective instrument of the Community.

Finally, Euratom's most spectacular failure was in its practically least important function, the production of indicative plans. Out of the 15 GW(e) nuclear generating capacity proposed for 1967 in *A Target for Euratom*, about 10 per cent was built and none was competitive with conventional sources. The targets were revised in the third General Report in 1960 and again in 1966 when Euratom as an institution proposed its first indicative programme.[47] The Commission based its demand forecast on the assumption that demand for electricity would rise more quickly than overall energy demand and that total energy demand would itself rise sharply; it based its case also on advances in nuclear technology and the maturity of the nuclear industry, which would both contribute to lower construction costs, on the use of enriched uranium in advanced reactors producing plutonium which in turn could be recycled, thus reducing fuel costs, and finally, on the commercial exploitation of fast reactors before 1980 – 180 GW(e) of fast reactor capacity was proposed for A.D. 2000.

The Commission produced incredibly optimistic estimates of the cost and performance of fast reactors which led them to predict that electricity demand would cost between 2 and 4 mills/kWh at 1966 price levels by A.D. 1985–2000. The targets proposed were:

	1960	1970	1980	1990	2000
Electricity consumption (TWh)	272	575	1080	1930	3450
Generating capacity (GW)	65	120	227	409	730
Minimum nuclear production (TWh)	—	28	280	920	2400
Minimum nuclear capacity (GW)	—	4	40	135	370

These estimates were raised the following year; the new target for 1980 was 60 GW(e) of nuclear capacity.

The timing of the first indicative programme, just before the merger of the Executives, was presumably intended to draw attention again to the nuclear option and establish the claim of Euratom to a say in the energy affairs of the merged Executives. It is doubtful if this intention was fulfilled because the credibility of Euratom was already low, and if its publications on energy policy about this time are compared with the publications of the Joint Executives it is clear that the influence of Euratom was not strong.

By the time the Executives were merged, Euratom had almost ceased to function as an institution; all that was left were the constituent parts, comprising the research centres, the Treaty and the personnel. These disembodied entities, without any real functional relationship, have nevertheless continued to affect community energy policy, much as chickens continue to run around after their heads have been cut off.

4. DEVELOPMENTS IN ELECTRICITY SUPPLY

One of the recommendations of the Benelux memorandum to the Messina conference had been that co-ordination of electricity supplies between states could reduce costs, and one of the three priorities of energy policy identified by the experts of the *Relance* Committee was a satisfactory method of meeting peak demands by pooling resources.

The supply of town gas and electricity on the continent at that time was in the hands of self-contained companies serving a small area. Each was obliged to install production capacity sufficient to serve the peak demand of his customers after due allowance for availability of plant. It was evident that interconnection of networks would permit demand to be met by a smaller total of installed capacity, partly because peak demands do not occur simultaneously everywhere, but mainly because in a larger network a smaller percentage margin of reserve capacity is needed to cope with breakdown and faulty prediction of demand.

In Europe negotiations between power suppliers have led to an international grid which now covers the entire continent. There is no doubt room for further improvement, but the chief mechanisms for co-operation and development, which are what matters in the present context, had been established by the end of the period now under discussion. It is an interesting story because the role of the EEC, and even of national governments, in the development of this international system of co-operation was negligible. Moreover, it would not be possible by looking at the European electricity transmission network or by studying its operation to detect the boundaries of the EEC. Indeed, in some ways the pivot of the system is Switzerland; one-quarter of the electricity produced in Switzerland is exported and she contributed 19 per cent of the total electricity exchanges in Western Europe in 1973, an amount quite out of proportion to the size of the country.

Co-operation between supply undertakings in Western Europe proceeds by joint consultation between neighbouring suppliers; these may be state controlled, such as *Electricité de France* (EDF) or *Ente Nazionale per l'Energia Elettrica* (ENEL), but in most cases they are private companies with only local ownership of generating and transmission equipment. National governments contributed by providing a legislative framework in which agreements to exchange electricity could be formulated, but the technical and organizational initiative came not from national governments, nor from the EEC Commission, but from international organizations set up by the electricity suppliers. The principal organizations established were

(a) Union for the Co-ordination of Production and Transport of Electricity (UCPTE) comprising the eight members of the West European network, i.e. Austria, Switzerland and the six Community countries;

(b) the International Union of Producers and Distributors of Electricity (called UNIPEDE from the initials of its French title) of which all European power suppliers are members.

Just as the oil companies designed a European oil supply and structure with little help from the Commission, so this essentially private endeavour designed a remarkably successful procedure for co-operation in electricity supply. It is sad that the Commission should again have lost the initiative to others in a matter that had been adopted by the European movement as long ago as the Messina conference. But although the diagnosis then had been good, the institutions devised were not capable of helping with the treatment.

D. Entr'acte

... despite [the Commission's] efforts none of these proposals has yet been approved by the [Council] although at the time they received a wide measure of assent from the European Parliament and from the Economic and Social Committee.

5th General Report, ECSC, EEC, EAEC, 1971.

The merging of the Executives, which took effect from 1 January 1967, was widely expected to promote a common energy policy. During the preceding months, the divided responsibility of the Executives for the various aspects of energy had frequently been cited as the reason why progress had been so slow. It was clearly essential for the prestige of the merged Executive that they do something to satisfy these expectations. As it happened, the merger was followed by the political crisis in the Middle East, the war in June 1967, the blockage of the Suez canal and the boycott of certain markets by Arab producers. The boycott was symbolic rather than real and the producers put little effort into ensuring that it was observed. Energy supplies to the Community were not seriously affected, but the events served dramatically to remind everyone of the insecurity of supply and further raised expectations of a common energy policy from the merged Executives. The time was ripe in all ways for an ambitious new initiative and the new Commission tried to take advantage of this. Unfortunately the preparation of the guidelines for the new comprehensive energy policy took up two years and much of the psychological impetus was lost. The only substantial new measure taken during 1967 and 1968 was to agree a directive that member states should stockpile 65 days supply of petroleum, the nation having the right of pre-emption; this followed an independent German initiative made two years previously.

The principal reason for the delay was the insistence of the Commissioner at the time (Herr Haferkamp) that proposals should be based on a solid analysis of the present and on short- and long-term guidelines for the future. The Commission also made some effort to sound out member states before publication by consulting expert bodies and by several sessions with COREPER. It was therefore not until December

1968 that the Commission submitted to the Council the *First Guidelines Towards a Community Energy Policy*.[48] This document was conceived as a political framework which the Commission would subsequently elaborate as an active policy by a series of specific proposals. In philosophical outlook it is possible to detect a significant shift away from the ideas prevalent in the ECSC, which had been the senior partner of the old joint working party, and towards the less protectionist attitude of the EEC. In substance the paper is a recapitulation and partial synthesis of the analyses already made for coal, hydrocarbons and nuclear power, with some shift in emphasis and presented as a consistent treatise held together by the final objective, which was to see the Treaty of Rome fully applied to energy.

The need for a common policy was predicated upon two principal grounds, the usual advantages of a common market and the special situation arising from the massive reliance on imports. The arguments ran that energy, unlike agriculture and industrial goods, was subject to uncoordinated national policies which distorted competition and prevented some regions of the Community from attracting investment. The dependence on imports was presented in a new light; the *Guidelines* argued that although it was undeniably a strategic weakness, it was also an opportunity for the Community to exert more influence in the world market by adopting a common approach.

The objectives of the common policy are the same as those of the 1964 Protocol, but the commitment to a low-cost energy policy is here made elaborately explicit. It is argued that the Treaties seek continued economic growth and improving standards of living for which cheap energy is essential. In a complete change of outlook, it is asserted that there is no conflict between low cost and security: 'The Community interest requires above all a secure supply at prices that are relatively stable and as low as possible. The assertion that this requirement contains a contradiction is not founded.' This assertion is followed by a sibylline gloss: 'It is only true that neither security nor low price can be attained absolutely.' One has very much the impression of a heresy rebuked.

The fundamental driving force of the policy was to be competition, although modified to a greater extent than would have been desirable elsewhere because of the need to prevent short-term interruptions of supply and to avoid entering into supply patterns that would in the long term be unsound. This wise intervention was to be seen as correcting distortions in competition that had crept in through peculiarities of the energy market; intervention would permit market forces to be more effective.

The *First Guidelines* also contained specific proposals. The Commission distinguished three families of proposal. The first family was intended to define a framework for action; it included a rolling five-year plan to serve as a guide to investment and proposals to intervene in the event of difficulties with supplies. The second family comprised technical proposals designed to establish a common market. The third family comprised proposals to promote cheap reliable supplies, mainly by intervention of the Commission to supervise and co-ordinate national policies. The chief regulators of the free market were to be:

community financial aids and a co-ordinated import policy to keep adequate indigenous production in being on the most competitive coalfields;
supervision of uranium, natural gas and oil supplies to make sure that the pattern offered as much security as was feasible; if not, the Commission would propose alterations;
co-ordination of investment; investments in energy were to be notified to the Commission which would compare them and give an opinion on their wisdom. If its recommendations were ignored then stronger measures would be proposed.

The Commission also proposed that the Community should help finance the exploration and production of hydrocarbons in circumstances that were of particular interest to the Community, and that a Community enterprise should be established to explore for and produce uranium both inside and outside the Community. The intention of these proposals was to obtain fuel supplies that were controlled by the Community. The Commission further proposed that the Supply Agency be returned to working condition, the better to permit the Commission to control supplies of nuclear fuel. In addition, the Community should help finance a variety of investments that might be in the common interest, but for which money might not otherwise be readily available.

There are two appendices: one, which is actually the bulk of the document, is a detailed account of the contemporary market for energy; in the second the Commission surveys the long-term perspective against which decisions should be set. It is reminiscent of earlier Euratom discussions of the importance of considering investments in the context of the distant future. The discussion asserts that consumers will turn to electricity for its convenience and efficiency; nuclear energy is singled out as being the form of primary energy most suited to Community policy; its cheapness and security are stressed – a perfect match for the objectives. '. . . nuclear energy is without doubt the best placed to reach in the given time the objectives of the energy policy.'

One can only speculate at the motives which underlay this initiative, but they may have been something along the following lines. The Commission sensibly recognized that it had lost the opportunity to give any immediate leadership in energy policy because it had been unable to influence to any significant extent the great European oil revolution. Moreover, in many respects it was ill-informed about what was going on in Europe, especially in the oil industry. Any attempt to assume a position of leadership would need to be made from a solid basis of information and understanding. The Annex in the *First Guidelines* describing the contemporary market was part of that attempt at understanding; nevertheless the Commission recognized that it was still inadequately informed and that it should become better informed both by regulations and by establishing personal contacts. The Commission was probably also impressed, like everyone else, by the oil companies' ability to handle the commercial consequences of the Middle East war and by the period of uninterrupted supplies since the Suez crisis in 1957, despite various potentially disruptive events. It probably concluded that there was no need to trade off cost and security, and that security could be achieved without appreciable cost by diversity and political co-operation. This was a convenient conclusion because it meant that the Community could benefit from low-cost oil in its homes and industries. Eventually the Commission would have hoped to give leadership by establishing a common market, which in practice would also have required a common supply policy and common pricing policies. In the meantime it would inform itself and obtain some prestige by finding solutions to particular problems within the Community, for example arranging the optimum design and use of gas pipeline networks crossing international borders.

The *First Guidelines* is the central document of Community energy policy. From a literary point of view it is simultaneously a union of everything that went before and the progenitor of almost everything to come. From an organizational point of view the work marks the transition from a specialist concern with the future of the coal industry to a concern with the competitive status of all forms of energy and the emphasis to be put on each. From a political point of view the *First Guidelines* is the first clear expression and justification of the comprehensive interventionist policy which the Commission has pursued ever since. From a practical point of view the immediate effect of the *Guidelines* was nil.

On the surface the lack of progress was the fault of the member states. It was not until November 1969, 11 months after they had received the *Guidelines*, that the Council met to discuss the document; this was the first Council meeting that had been devoted to energy since the Executives had been merged almost three years previously. The Council approved the fundamental principles of the *Guidelines* and asked for concrete proposals as soon as possible. The Council had already one proposal on freedom of establishment in prospecting; the Commission now sent to it:

49

a proposal that the Commission be notified of imports of crude oil and oil products in order that it might keep track of the supply of hydrocarbons to the Community and ensure that the pattern offered adequate security;

proposals that firms be obliged to notify the Commission in confidence of investment projects for the production, transport, storage and distribution of electricity and hydrocarbons;

a proposal to set an upper limit on excise duties on fuel;

a proposal to amend the Euratom Treaty to strengthen the Supply Agency;

a proposal that firms in the member states should be encouraged to co-operate in joint enterprises of Community interest in return for tax concessions and attractive loans;

a proposal that the Commission be given authority to raise loans for a Community contribution to the finance of power stations;

a proposal to extend oil stocks to the equivalent of 90 days supply;

a proposal requiring owners to offset transport in pipelines crossing frontiers on non-discriminatory terms.

These proposals were the elements of the policy of little steps; none of them had been accepted by the Council by the end of 1971; the Commission complained that 'despite its efforts none of these proposals has yet been approved by the [Council] although at the time they received a wide measure of assent from the European Parliament and the Economic and Social Committee'. The plaintive note is in sharp contrast to the old castigations of the High Authority.

The only development of substance up to the end of 1971 was to prolong the Community system of aid to the coal industry. The basis of the procedure was modified slightly; member states were authorized to grant aid for the closure of pits, capital investment, training and stockpiling. The grand strategy, to which practice was supposed to conform, was to adapt coal output to market conditions by concentrating on the most productive mines. The Commission was to be supplied with full information and justification and had to authorize the aid. Inevitably though, as the member states were putting up their own money for their own industries, the authorization by the Commission was a formality.

During 1972 the Council approved a directive increasing the mandatory stocks of oil to 90 days and finally approved the regulations for notifying imports of hydrocarbons and investment projects. The Commission made proposals for more little steps:

a proposal that member states should equip themselves with the powers to intervene in the energy market in the event of difficulties in supply;

a proposal to establish common arrangements for imports of hydrocarbons from non member states;
a proposal for a new system of aid for coking coal and coke, similar
in principle to the temporary scheme expiring in December 1972.

But these came to nothing.

In the five years from the merger of the Executives to the end of 1972
there was no significant step towards a common energy policy. Even
such matters as were agreed were extensions of initiatives made years
before and therefore required the minimum of political will; the Community system of state aids was extended, the volume of mandatory oil
stocks was increased and the obligation to notify the Commission of
imports and investments was extended from the coal and nuclear sectors
to hydrocarbons.

Explanations for this poor performance generally attribute blame to
two factors, the lack of political will among member states and lack of
leadership from the Commission. These criticisms are evidently wide
enough to encompass the truth whatever it might be. To be useful it is
necessary to be more precise.

The lack of any interest in energy policy from the member states is
certainly the most striking aspect of the period. The first meeting of the
Council to be dedicated to energy took place nearly three years after
the Executives had been merged and nearly a year after the Commission's comprehensive study had been published. Even thereafter discussion of energy was desultory and there was no determination to
reach agreement. There was, in fact, agreement in principle on many
of these proposals, but there was no determination to solve the secondary problems that they threw up. For example, there was disagreement
on what minimum size of investment should be notified and how the
information should be presented; the Dutch, being the home of the
Royal Dutch Shell, were reluctant to enforce the disclosure of information about the intentions of private firms. The reason for the lack
of determination was not so much that the proposals would have harmed
the interests of member states, but much more that no member state
felt it had anything to gain from the proposals, and therefore no government made an effort to have them agreed.

The time was also generally a time of great complacency about oil
supplies. The crisis in the Middle East had in the end been seen not as
evidence of a threat to supplies of oil, but more as evidence that whatever happened the Middle Eastern oil producers would watch out that
their commercial interests were not harmed. The record of reliable oil
supplies at ever-decreasing price was entirely satisfactory to member
states and they saw no reason to make any effort to construct a common energy policy. It is interesting to note in passing that 1967 was

also the date of the White Paper on Fuel Policy in the United Kingdom[49] which shared the confident opinion on the scarcity of oil supplies.

The final constituent of this lack of political will was the essential similarity of the member states. It had been argued at the time that the Executives were merged that the energy economies of the member states were becoming rapidly more alike; that the old distinction and conflict of interests between the coal producing countries and the energy deficient countries was disappearing and that the road to a common policy would be smoothed. This is probably to misunderstand the forces that are necessary to create a common policy against the inevitable inertia of nationalism; the point is analysed at length later, but briefly it seems that if all countries are similarly endowed there is little scope for specialization and the benefits of economic integration are small. Conflict of interest is then the prerequisite of any situation from which a common policy can evolve; strong interest and expectation of gain from at least one member state is also essential. These particular tensions being absent from 1967 until the United Kingdom joined the Community in January 1973, it is no surprise that the Council of Ministers found little to interest them in energy.

It is less easy to learn anything from the charge that the Commission showed no leadership. It is certainly true that it did not, but it had little opportunity. It is doubtful, in fact, if the Commission can lead when the member states have no interest. It is often said that the Commission (in particular Signor Mansholt) showed great leadership in the common agricultural policy, but in that instance leadership took the form of mediating between powerful national interests; there were at least strong forces to influence. In the absence of similar interests in energy there was perhaps little that the Commission could do. The only force which might have moulded a common policy at that stage was a threat from outside. The Commission chose to give up the opportunity of exploiting the potential threat in the dependence on oil supplies by minimizing the whole business of security. In doing this it was, in effect, creating a policy for the past seven years during which oil had been extraordinarily reliable. The doctrine of compatibility of low cost and security only passed into Commission thinking on energy as it was in fact ceasing to hold. The Commission were not alone in this judgement, but it is nevertheless true that they might have judged otherwise; their writings in this period are full of the consequences of depending on such large imports of energy, but they never tried in practice to use this weakness as a possible incentive to member states to try to agree a common policy.

Eventually, disgruntled by the lack of progress, the Commission decided to present its policy in a new and more dramatic form, which it did by means of Herr Haferkamp's famous 46 points. Although essentially faithful to the policy presented in 1968, the Commission took the opportunity to bring the *Guidelines* up to date. The initiative was presented to the Council in October 1972 as two documents: *Problems and Means of the Energy Policy for 1975–1985* is an analysis of the Commission's position in the energy market and a prognosis for the next 12 to 13 years; *Necessary Progress in Community Energy Policy* contains the 46 points and supporting logic.[50,51]

The energy market was seen to have changed since 1968, most importantly because of the changed attitude of exporting countries evident in the Teheran and Tripoli agreements of 1971 and the general drift to a sellers' market in energy. It was recognized that decisions taken by the U.S.A., Japan and the U.S.S.R. would affect the Community and that energy supply could only be effectively handled if it were seen and treated as an international affair. Analysis of these, and other changes, 'lead first of all to a remarkable confirmation of the fundamental theses of the *First Guidelines*', but the emphasis has shifted. Stronger powers of intervention were recommended to ensure that the trend to horizontal and vertical integration, particularly by the oil companies, but also by state enterprises, did not prejudice a balanced competitive industrial structure, and also to ensure adequate investment both in terms of volume and allocation. Similarly the relation between energy policy, commercial, economic and foreign policy and Europe's trading balance was seen to justify some central control.

Resolute development of nuclear energy and more imports of natural gas are proposed, these fuels being cited to confound the heresy that security and low cost are incompatible. There is also detailed discussion of the special relationship between Europe and the Middle East; extensive commercial, industrial and technological co-operation are recommended to promote political stability. This was the first time that much had been made of this in Commission analysis, although it was an old idea of the OEEC.[18]

The detailed proposals are mainly of two classes; one comprises general exhortations as to what should be done, for example better methods of exploration should be found; the other comprises proposals already put without success to the Council and adds some more intended to obtain information on pricing policies and reserves; the Commission realized that prices were determined by factors which varied from energy source to energy source and might not be an adequate measure of competition; they wished therefore to know how these prices were established; they also wished to know the extent of proven, probable and possible reserves of oil and gas and the technical and financial prospects for the exploitation of these fields. For the first time also it is suggested that the Community have right of pre-emption on natural gas extracted from the North Sea and, though there is no specific suggestion, it is mentioned in passing that member states might be obliged to exploit petroleum reserves to the profit of the Community.

These documents were perhaps a little more interventionist than the *Guidelines* and the supporting logic was brought up to date, but in most respects Herr Haferkamp's swan song differed little from his overture.

In the same month as these documents were published, a summit conference was held in Paris between the Heads of State of the existing member states of the Communities and of the three states due to join in 1973. The summit demanded 'as soon as possible an energy policy guaranteeing certain and lasting supplies under satisfactory economic conditions'. This reference to energy policy is reported to have been included at the instigation of Mr. Heath, partly because he did not share the general complacency about energy supplies and partly because he thought that the United Kingdom might have something to contribute; no one could have divined what contribution the United Kingdom was going to make.

E. Sound and Fury

> ... it is a tale
> Told by an idiot, full of sound and fury,
> Signifying nothing.
> *Macbeth*, Act V, Scene V.

When the Community was enlarged to include the United Kingdom, Ireland and Denmark, the composition of the Commission and the responsibilities of the Commissioners changed; M. Simonet became Commissioner for energy. He was faced with two specific matters requiring urgent attention, a dispute over coking-coal subsidies and an attempt to throttle Euratom, and with the general obligation to prosecute the initiative of the 46 points.

The old system of aids to the Community coking-coal industry had expired at the end of 1972 before the Council of Ministers had agreed on a replacement. The German steelmakers were furious because they were constrained by their national government to buy Community coke and forbidden to import from third countries; in practice this meant they were obliged to use German coke. Other Community steelmakers were under no such obligation and were therefore able to import coke from America and Australia at prices up to 15 DM per tonne below the price of German coke. This difference had existed for many years but the consequences were at the time exacerbated by a recession in the steel industry; moreover, all the signs were that the difference would increase rapidly in the future. German coke benefited from a subsidy of about 5 DM per tonne, but this still left the German steel industry at a disadvantage. The existing subsidy consisted of two elements, one paid for by the producing government, one paid out of a Community fund. The Commission proposed to continue the system in principle, but to increase both subsidies and change the method of financing the Community subsidy; the money was to be raised in future by a levy on the steel industry according to the quantity of coking coal used. Essentially this was a subsidy from the whole Community steel industry to the German coking-coal industry. Not surprisingly the Netherlands and Italy, with their coastal steel sites, vigorously opposed the idea; the United Kingdom was also against it because, although a producer of coking coal, she also imported large quantities and stood on balance to lose more than she gained. The German Government supported the proposals, although within Germany the interests of the coking-coal industry and the steel industry conflicted – the steel industry going so far as to offer to buy back the coking-coal mines, which had once belonged to them, if they could then close them down. The affair was important to the Commission because it was the only commercial trans- action within the energy market where the states had done more than co-ordinate their policies and had undertaken common action. Eventu- ally, after several meetings of the Council, a system of Community subsidy was agreed in July 1973, although the Dutch manifested their dissent by abstaining on the vote.

British entry came close to destroying the Euratom research agencies. At the time the Euratom budget was less than one-fifth of one per cent of the money being spent in the Community on nuclear matters, which is some indication of how ineffective has been the attempt to make this a common endeavour. But France and the United Kingdom reckoned that this was still too much for the benefit they were getting; they demanded a large reduction in the budget. For a time it was believed that Euratom might be scrapped, but eventually, thanks largely to a vigorous defence by the Commission, a research budget was agreed.

Although it was important for the Commission to preserve what remnants it could of the achievements of the past, it had also to persist with its new initiative to create a comprehensive policy for the future. The psychological environment was favourable. The American energy crisis, which had long been predicted, was becoming manifest in the closure of schools for lack of heating oil and the restriction of airline services for lack of fuel. This energy crisis was really the result of a few specific actions and not fundamental; a shortage of refinery capacity in the U.S.A., plus the delayed effects of savage price control, had brought the supply of refined products below demand; American demand spilled over into Europe and caused amazingly high prices in the small Rotterdam spot market. The possibility of having permanently to import large quantities of oil from the Middle East had brought the

U.S.A. the cares of insecure supplies that had afflicted Europe for a long time and which Europe had learned to accept and even ignore. A speech from President Nixon on American energy supplies was rumoured. The uncertainty transferred itself to Europe, both the psychological anxiety and the practical uncertainty of what consequences in Europe might follow from changes in supplies to America.

The Commission recast the essentials of its ideas into *Guidelines and Priority Activities*[52] ready to be discussed by the Council in May at a meeting to be devoted to energy policy. The meeting lasted 19 hours, paid little attention to the bulk of the Commission's proposals, was devoted principally to oil, apparently led to agreement, but in reality revealed the profound differences of opinion which have paralysed Community energy policy ever since.

The main dissension was between member states who argued that energy policy should start from a common internal policy – in particular common regulation of the oil market – and those states who argued that energy policy began from a common front to the world outside. Within this dissension were the seeds of the still more profound difference of opinion that later was to be responsible for much of the disorganized response of consuming nations to the oil producers – the difference of opinion between those countries, chiefly France, who believed in dialogue and those countries who preferred consumer solidarity. The Commission considered this a false dilemma and proposed to do both concurrently.

The member states agreed in principle that oil supplies were an international matter and that discussion with America and Japan was necessary, as also were approaches to producing countries. But France argued that a common internal policy for prices and imports had priority over the definition of a Community attitude and, indeed, was the first and inescapable step to that end. The other countries were in varying degrees unenthusiastic about regulation of the internal market. Denmark and Germany were against government control in principle, and strong German resistance was therefore expected, but she turned out to be surprisingly willing to compromise; later in the year she began to devise her own oil policy around her own national oil company, which is partly state-owned. The Netherlands and the United Kingdom were strongly opposed to control because they were the home of international oil companies, from whose uncontrolled operations they expected benefits in excess of anything they were likely to gain from control. France and Italy exercised tight control over their own oil industries and therefore had in principle no objection to co-ordinated control.

All states were agreed on the benefits of a common procedure for imports and exports, but France and Italy, and probably the Commission, thought this was only feasible within a supply policy that covered the fixing of prices as well.

On balance most countries preferred to go straight to a common external policy, and eschewed common internal control. The French argued that the Community had no authority under the Treaties to act in this way, that it could not define a common position to the outside world. Not for the first time, French scruples about the Treaties conveniently coincided with the independent actions she wished to take within her own foreign policy; she wanted to keep her hands free for her own dealings in the Middle East and probably also did not want to give the Commission any authority to deal with the U.S.A., with whom French relations were cool. In the end the Commission was left with little agreement of substance on either matter.

The Council did agree on some politically less-sensitive matters. It approved a directive that member states would provide themselves with powers to take necessary measures in the event of difficulties with oil supply; the states bound themselves to designate the bodies responsible for implementing the measures and to prepare intervention plans to distribute stocks, restrain consumption, decide priorities and control prices. They also agreed that the Community could give financial support to ventures considered of fundamental importance in ensuring its supply of hydrocarbons, and that a Committee should be set up, the Standing Committee on Uranium Enrichment (COPENUR), to keep up to date on uranium enrichment, recommend on Community needs, and co-ordinate work. This latter decision was a compromise; the Council had been asked to give an opinion on a proposal for the member states in common to build a plant for enriching uranium. The United Kingdom-German-Dutch 'troika' preferred the centrifugal process, the French preferred the diffusion process. The Council recognized that it was an important matter, not least because of the higher prices and fiercer terms of the contracts for fuel with the Atomic Energy Commission in Washington which provided Europe at the time, and still does, with most of her supplies. But the Council felt unable to judge the technology, so COPENUR was set up to advise them. In fact, the 'troika' and France were both committed by previous investment and prestige to their chosen technology and no recommendation from a committee was likely to change that, but the device did serve to hide disagreement temporarily.

The *Guidelines and Priority Activities* contained no concrete commitments and therefore the Council was able to approve them as an appropriate basis for further discussions; it also 'noted with satisfaction the Commission's intention to submit to it ... concrete proposals regarding the Community energy policy'.[53] But in fact the meeting had failed to grasp a favourable opportunity for Community action.

57

There are several reasons for this. The desultory meetings on energy in the preceding five years had failed to make any progress towards agreement on the common regulation of the oil industry; the topic remained a genuine matter of contention and a most suitable scapegoat within the confines of energy policy to bear the blame for incompatible attitudes in a wider arena. Oil had always been an important aspect of foreign policy for European states, especially of the policy of France and the United Kingdom in the Middle East. France believed that she had more to gain from independent diplomacy in the Middle East than from participation in a consumer grouping which would restrict her actions elsewhere. Given the hidden disagreement in the wider context there was little that a meeting of Energy Ministers could have achieved. Indeed, it is said that the French delegates were working from a brief that came directly from President Pompidou.[54]

During the summer the Commission continued to pursue its joint objectives of a regulated internal market and a common external policy; the latter concept was never well defined but it presumably meant any show of solidarity such as oil sharing. In August 1973 the Commission submitted to the Council six proposals that went some way towards creating a common internal market. The effect of these proposals would have been:

to inform the Commission about imports of oil products and exports of all hydrocarbons, in other words, a system of supervision;

to set up a hydrocarbon supply committee in which member states and the Commission could discuss under what circumstances intervention in the activities of the oil companies might be agreed;

to set up a common system of imports and exports so that intervention could be executed and co-ordinated;

to harmonize fuel oil taxes.

But nothing came of even these modest proposals; the initiative of the 46 points had been buried by the Council in May.

The aftermath of the Yom Kippur war put great stress on the Community. On 17 October 1973 the Arab countries threatened to cut their combined production of oil by 5 per cent immediately and to continue to reduce production thereafter until Israel withdrew from the occupied Arab lands. In December 1973 the oil producing countries stopped fixing the price of crude oil in agreement with the oil companies and decided that in future they would fix them unilaterally. Subsequently the price of crude oil delivered in Community ports rose to more than three times its price before the war and five times its price before the Teheran-Tripoli agreements. These changes had severe effects on the world economy. In particular, they removed the competitive advantage that Europe had held over the U.S.A. in its access to cheap energy. The

political stresses, however, had the most immediate effect. The oil pro
ducers in the Middle East issued an embargo against the Netherlands,
whom the Community promptly and publicly abandoned; governments
of member states made no attempt to share oil supplies, what sharing
did take place being organized by oil companies; France and the United
Kingdom sought privileged access to oil in the Middle East; and in
November the Foreign Ministers of the Community took a joint stand
in favour of the Arab states, a position that was confirmed by the
Heads of Government at a summit meeting in Copenhagen in December.

During this time the first priority of the Commission was to keep the
common market intact and avoid member states taking unauthorized
national measures. In effect this meant that the Commision was prepared to condone almost any action, provided that it was first notified
to the Commission so that it could be authorized and the form preserved. The Commission also approached the Council with proposals
for oil sharing, but some member states, especially the United Kingdom,
resisted the idea. Provoked by this prevarication, the Commission sent
a package of proposals direct to the December summit meeting in
Copenhagen. It was hoped that the summit would have the authority
to arrange a compromise between two sectors, the Germans paying
through the regional fund for United Kingdom co-operation in oil
sharing, but neither Germany nor the United Kingdom would co-
operate and the attempt only served to inflame the mutual hostility that
prevailed at the time.

The summit was accounted a political success in that, spurred on by
the Arab solidarity appropriately incarnated in Copenhagen by a delegation from the Algiers summit, the Community presented a semblance
of a common front and issued a joint statement on the Middle East
crisis favourable to the Arab cause. The compromise was assisted by
covert support to the Netherlands from other member states. The
Heads of State also affirmed their political will to agree a common
energy policy and asked the Commission to submit proposals; they
took, however, no practical steps.

The common public front was short-lived; there was open disagreement in the following Council of Foreign Ministers. The Commission
had presented proposals[55,56] aimed at ensuring that all member states
should take steps to cut down oil and energy consumption in accordance
with uniform criteria, and that they should share information and
scrutinize prices to make sure that the oil companies were not taking
advantage of the situation. The United Kingdom was unenthusiastic
about these proposals; being the home of two oil companies, she was
prepared to see the companies distribute available supplies. Germany
retaliated by refusing to augment the regional fund and the United
Kingdom blocked subsequent discussions on energy policy. At the end

of January the United Kingdom withdrew her opposition and the Council agreed some of the less sensitive measures, for providing the Commission with information necessary to draw up energy balance sheets, and for setting up an Energy Committee of senior national government officials, chaired by the Commission, that would be responsible for implementing any measures adopted by the Council.

The affirmation by the summit meeting in Copenhagen of the political will of the member states to agree a common energy policy was the formal source of a new, and most recent, Commission initiative. The formulation and especially the prosecution of this initiative took place amid a bewildering variety of attempts to organize international dialogues between and amongst producers and consumers. The sudden promotion of energy policy to an international affair of first rank has greatly influenced progress towards a Community energy policy. It is necessary, therefore, to give a brief account of the activity in this wider arena before considering the activities of the Community itself.

Events were dominated by three principal conflicts of interest within the industrial nations. The concept dear to Europeans of a special relationship with the Middle East conflicted with the desire of other industrial nations to see Europe subsumed into the general class of consumers. The need for a meeting of consumers and producers of oil was widely perceived; France and the U.S.A. struggled for the diplomatic laurels and prestige of organizing the affair and for the real benefits of thereby shaping its form and outcome. The Community had difficulty in presenting the conflicting interests of its member states within a single mandate.

At the December summit the European Heads of Government agreed that the Community should try to develop the old idea of a special relationship with the Arab world through what was to be known as the Euro-Arab dialogue. This initiative was matched almost simultaneously by Dr. Kissinger's proposal that Japan, the U.S.A. and the nations of Western Europe should form a joint energy action group. The idea that the great oil importing areas of the present (Europe and Japan) and the near future (the U.S.A.) should talk together and with the oil producing nations about ways of stabilizing the market had been current in Europe and the U.S.A. well before the Yom Kippur war; official discussions between Europe and the U.S.A. date at least from M. Simonet's visit to Washington in May 1973. Dr. Kissinger's proposal was well received by the Community countries, even by the United Kingdom and, apparently, by France, the independent efforts of these countries to negotiate favoured-nation treatment with the Arab producers not having been strikingly successful up to that time.

The first of these initiatives to take practical form was that of the U.S.A. A conference of industrial nations was convened in Washington in February 1974. In preparation for the conference the Commission drafted a Community mandate to the President of the Commission and the Chairman of the Council of Ministers that they might attend the conference as representatives of the Community. In deference to France the draft insisted that the oil producing countries and the third world should be included in any subsequent discussions; the French argued that the grouping of industrial nations should be treated as a partner in a dialogue, rather than as a cartel of consumers. The mandate also made it clear that the Community retained its right to confer independently with the Middle East.

A principal result of the Washington conference was to identify the sharp difference of opinion between France and the other participants. France declared herself against any joint action by industrial nations that might be construed as aggression. The final communiqué of the conference was signed by all participants except France; that is, by the U.S.A., Canada, Japan, Norway and eight Community countries; it committed the signatories to joint action in the conservation of energy, the development of new sources, research and development and oil sharing; this was to be done within a group known as the Energy Co-ordination Group (ECG). The communiqué also put tentatively into print some sign of the widespread distrust of the oil companies which, always latent, had flared up after October 1973; the signatories agreed to examine in detail the role of the international oil companies, by which was meant their pricing policies, tax behaviour and possible collusion in the energy crisis. France rejected oil sharing in principle as aggressive. By then French confidence had been bolstered by some limited success in arranging bilateral deals with oil producers; she was also sceptical about the extent to which signatories would stand by the agreement in a new crisis; in short, she saw no reason to abandon the benefits of bilateral deals for the dubious advantages of joint confrontation. Also, France recognized that the ECG was partly a device whereby the U.S.A. could be sure of directing the attempts of the industrialized non-communist world to adapt to the oil crisis and she insisted, to her credit, that European interests were not necessarily identical to the interests of the U.S.A., nor advanced by American protection.

The signatories to the communiqué also agreed to hold a conference between the industrial nations and the producers as soon as possible. Meanwhile, sub-groups were established dealing with oil, uranium, conservation, research and development, and the oil companies; their job was to sort out some common attitudes.

An oil sharing plan was submitted to the ECG by Kissinger in the autumn of 1974, along with proposals to guarantee high-cost investment in new energy sources if oil prices should fall. The basis of the oil sharing scheme was that member countries should keep stocks, control demand

61

and conserve energy. If one country was deprived of oil to the extent of 5 per cent of its previous year's supply, then the rest would share both imported and home-produced oil with the afflicted member. If supply to the whole group dropped by 5 per cent, then members would be obliged to cut demand. The provisions would operate automatically. The proposal was agreed in principal in the ECG, but later attempts by the U.S.A. to get formal agreement showed that amongst some of the nations with oil of their own, especially the United Kingdom, Canada and Norway, enthusiasm had waned. Eventually a similar scheme was agreed; the main change was that the provisions were not to be automatic but would depend on a vote.

In November 1974 the grouping of industrial nations was converted to an agency of the OECD, the International Energy Agency (IEA). Most countries of the OECD are members, the principal exception being France. The highest decision-making body of the agency is a governing board composed of ministers or their delegates assisted by a secretariat. It is an interesting international organization in that it can make majority decisions on a few important matters which are then binding on members. To French eyes, and some others, it appeared that members of the IEA were being asked to concede a degree of sovereignty to an institution inspired and largely controlled by the U.S.A.

Although under great pressure from her partners, France refused to join the IEA. This decision presented a great problem to the Commission; its ramifications have exercised the ingenuity of the Commission's officials ever since. The sharing of oil in a crisis with other IEA countries but not France would be against the general principles of a common market and the specific Article 34 of the Treaty of Rome which forbids quantitative restrictions on trade between member states. The Commission tried to set up an identical oil sharing scheme within the EEC, to make France in practice, but not in name, a member of the IEA, but France then and since would have nothing to do with oil sharing.

The formation of the IEA without France also prevented the Commission from advancing any claim to represent the Community within the IEA, which would have enhanced the Commission's prestige; instead it was obliged to accept a co-ordinating role of minor significance. In this instance France reinforced her objections to oil sharing with the argument that the Community needed a common energy policy before it could sensibly act in concert with other consumers.

Meanwhile attempts to further the Community's own initiative, the Euro-Arab dialogue, had been going on almost continuously since June 1974; they were, however, thwarted, first by the Arab countries' demands that the Palestine Liberation Organization be represented, and then by Arab objections to a Community trade agreement with Israel.

Eventually a preliminary meeting opened in June 1975. Both sides wanted a platform from which to posture: the Arabs wanted to expose their grievances about the Palestine question; the Europeans wanted to demonstrate the special relationship existing between the two regions. The Europeans were anxious to avoid talking about Middle Eastern politics, both so as not to infringe on U.S. territory and because it was bad for trade. Little progress was made.

In March 1975 the fragile unity of the IEA was tested by Dr. Kissinger's reiteration of his proposal to protect investment in energy production in the industrial nations by introducing a minimum support price (MSP), or floor price, for oil. Most member states had little interest in protecting United Kingdom or U.S.A. high-cost energy and at the same time protecting OPEC. An MSP seemed to most delegations a more suitable objective for a cartel of producers. Unsurprisingly, the proposal for an MSP of $9 per barrel was supported only by the United Kingdom and Norway. Benefiting from this distraction within the IEA and the hostility of the Arab states to this agency and its chief sponsor (a preliminary meeting of the industrial nations and the Arab states to organize a producer-consumer dialogue within the IEA had led to nothing but mutual recrimination) France managed to steal the initiative and become host to the dialogue by inviting consumers and producers to Paris. The oil producers insisted that the conference be tripartite, comprising industrial nations, oil producing nations and developing countries; they insisted also that the agenda should include not only oil, but food, raw materials, trade and finance. In other words the conference would cover the economies of the non-communist world – it became known as the North-South dialogue. At a preparatory meeting in October 1975 the industrial nations granted these requests. Commissions studying energy (not oil), raw materials, development and finance were set up with equal representation from the oil producers, industrial nations and developing countries.

The United Kingdom had made it known from the time the North-South dialogue was mooted that she would not accept representation by a Community delegation except in such matters as the Community had agreed beforehand, and that she insisted on representing herself for the matter of North Sea oil. At the summit meeting in Rome in December 1975 the other member states without exception disagreed strongly with this demand. After some unfriendly debate, the United Kingdom abandoned its claim to a separate seat; in return France appeared to accept the principle of an MSP and to reconsider its refusal to join an oil sharing scheme. The only actual commitment by France in the communiqué was to seek 'protective mechanisms' for new energy sources; the United Kingdom chose to represent this as a commitment to an MSP. In fact, the United Kingdom Government must have

63

realized that no such concession had been made or it would have been clearly formulated in the communiqué. Presumably all they could get in return for abandoning the claim to a separate seat was a meaningless formula, which could be presented temporarily as a concession of substance to the constituency at home.

The North-South dialogue finally opened in December 1975, and the Commissions began negotiations which have continued ever since. The inaugural meeting of the Euro-Arab dialogue at last began in May 1976.

Little of substance has been achieved.

In February 1976, in Paris, the IEA finally agreed an MSP of $7 a barrel as part of their long-term strategy to lessen dependence on imported oil. The member states also committed themselves to measures to strengthen conservation of energy, research and development, and exploitation of new sources. The MSP was pressed by the energy rich countries, the U.S.A., the United Kingdom, Canada and Norway; it was only accepted by the energy deficient countries on the understanding that the member states of the IEA would make oil available without any restrictions, such as tariff penalties or export quotas. This posed problems for Canada, because of its federal structure and the existence of restrictions in some of its states; the accord could only become effective after these restrictions on access had been lifted. The agreement has yet to be ratified by the member governments.

Then, in April 1976, another international agreement on energy matters was presented to the public, after several secret meetings. This time it concerned fissile material. Ever since the explosion of the first atomic bomb, the U.S.A. had been trying to control the proliferation of nuclear weapons. Several recent events had shown that its control was slipping; India exploded a nuclear device, West Germany agreed to sell enrichment and reprocessing technology to Brazil, and France began negotiations with Pakistan and South Korea for the same purpose. In April 1975 the U.S.A. convened a secret meeting in London between the U.S.S.R., the U.S.A., the United Kingdom, Canada, Japan, West Germany and France. A year later the seven nuclear-exporting countries announced the non-binding agreement to control and supervise the use of nuclear technology and materials. Because the agreement involved three Community countries, who pledged themselves in essence not to operate a free market in nuclear materials within the Community, it was construed by the remaining Community countries as infringing the EAEC Treaty. This accusation has not been pressed because the practical significance of the agreement will probably be small. But in so far as Community countries once more sought a solution to their problems outside the Community, the affair was yet another discouragement to a European energy policy.

This was the foreign policy environment in which the Community energy policy had to be developed. We return now to the Commission's attempts to prepare a new energy strategy after the Yom Kippur war and the ritual expression of political will at the Copenhagen summit.

The published version[57] of the new strategy begins with an analysis of the implications of the crisis, identifies the vulnerable points in the supply pattern, and concludes that the aim of the strategy must be to make fundamental changes in that pattern in order to reduce the dependence on oil. 'The experience of the latter part of 1973 *must . . .* be an incentive to the Community to reduce its dependence for energy on the rest of the world *to the utmost extent possible.*'[58] But equal stress is put on cheapness of supply: 'the energy sources must be available at the lowest possible price as an incentive to potential users'.[59]

It is asserted that 'nuclear energy . . . is the only acceptable alternative to oil open to the Community'. Targets are set for the various sectors of the energy economy in 1985. The rational use of energy is to reduce consumption in 1985 by 15 per cent from the estimates made before the oil crisis.[51] Nuclear power capacity for generation of electricity is to be increased some fourteenfold to 200 GW by 1985, and the installation of an additional 20 GW(e) is recommended for supplying space heat and industrial-process heat. Natural gas and oil production in the Community is to be increased as rapidly and by as much as is physically possible, imports of natural gas are to be increased, indigenous coal production is to be maintained and supplies of oil diversified. Imported fuels are not to exceed 40 per cent of the total consumption in 1985.

The original draft also provided for an EEC energy agency financed by a levy on energy imports. The revenue would be used to finance the construction of nuclear power stations and to carry out research and development in products that could help the Community achieve greater independence in energy supply. The proposal was watered down to anticipate objections from the United Kingdom, and although the concept of a supranational agency was retained, the deletion of any satisfactory statement of its functions gives the impression that the concept had not been thought through.

The strategy stands in continuity with the *First Guidelines,*[48] but the emphasis has shifted in one crucial respect. The principal concern of the *First Guidelines* is with the present; the aim is to ensure competition and a free market; intervention in the market is seen as supervision to improve its working. The practical proposals arising out of that initiative were mainly directed to obtaining the information on trade, investment and pricing that would be necessary for intelligent supervision of the market. It is implied, although never put so crudely, that if a vigorous, competitive market can be constructed now, then the future will look after itself. The survey of the long-term perspective, which contains the traditional Euratom arguments about preparing for the future, is banished to the Second Annexe.

In contrast, the New Strategy implies that the discontinuous change in oil prices had made the existing pattern of energy supply quite inappropriate (or sub optimum). In order to organize the transition to a new optimum, it was essential to have a vision of the future towards which the Community should work. It was necessary, therefore, to adopt a view on what the potential of alternative sources of energy might be and which of them should be promoted. Ever since its inception, Euratom had preached the imperative need to take into account the long-term evolution of the structure of energy supplies. After this sudden shift of emphasis away from immediate market conditions onto the future structure of supply, it was inevitable that the Commission should adopt and adapt the views that had been current for so long in Euratom and were ready to hand. Hence the conclusion that nuclear energy was the only acceptable alternative to oil.

The strategy was enthusiastically endorsed by the European Parliament, the Economic and Social Committee, the ECSC Consultative Committee and the Energy Committee; it was submitted to the Council in July 1974. Consultation within COREPER and the Energy Committee had encouraged hopes that the strategy would be agreed unanimously. In the end, the Commission and eight member states agreed a resolution approving the voluntary objectives and the need to restructure energy supply and demand, but the United Kingdom refused to accept the resolution, on the grounds that it was being asked to approve principles and guidelines without it being clear what were the practical consequences. France would not accept an amputated resolution, and in the end the meeting produced nothing of substance. This was a disaster for the Commission; they had been denied the symbolic expression of political will and, therefore, any basis for submitting concrete proposals. The momentum of the Commission's effort was lost. The United Kingdom made it plain that she considered the Energy Co-ordination Group to be the important forum; this was, in itself, a serious matter for the Commission, because if member states prefer to seek solutions outside the Community, it is both a sign and a cause of the weakening of the Community.

Eventually an amputated resolution was agreed in September, affirming 'political resolve to formulate and implement a common energy policy'. The United Kingdom succeeded in deleting from the resolution the suggestion that the Community should speak with a single voice in discussing these problems with the outside world. Even so, the change of United Kingdom opinion was unexpected; it almost certainly followed the considerable pressure put on the United Kingdom Prime Minister at the 'Elysée dinner' a few days before.

One would like to think that the original United Kingdom refusal to accept the resolution was based on the sensible case it actually presented. The targets were unrealistic, the extent of participation of each state and the allocation of responsibility for achieving the targets were quite obscure. However, if the United Kingdom really based its action on this case, it should have done so before the Council meeting was held and not encouraged others to think it would agree. Much goodwill, painfully acquired, was lost as a result. The reasons for not accepting the resolution were more probably that the Minister acting for the United Kingdom was not enthusiastic about the Community, the political party in power was busy constructing a public posture appropriate to the forthcoming referendum, and the Council meeting suffered.

At the September meeting, discussion of the targets was postponed until December. In preparation for this meeting, the Commission produced the most detailed analysis of policy that it has yet made. It comprises a series of documents setting out the general objectives of policy and the supporting background and logic.[60-67] Essentially, these are an elaboration and justification of the 'New Strategy' and not new thinking. Minor changes were made to the objectives for 1985; in particular, the 20 GW(e) of nuclear capacity for process heat in 1985 is dropped. The supporting documents, particularly for electricity supply and nuclear fuel,[61,62] extend their discussion to A.D. 2000.

At the December meeting the Council adopted a resolution in which the objectives suggested by the Commission were reduced to a sum of the contemporary plans of member states. The main changes were the objectives for nuclear capacity (160 GW(e) by 1985 and, if possible, 200 GW(e)) and imports (50 per cent by 1985 and, if possible, 40 per cent). The Council also approved a resolution on the rational use of energy, which bound them to try to consume 15 per cent less energy in 1985 than the amount forecast for that date in January 1973. The resolution will doubtless be observed, but because of errors in the original forecast and higher energy prices, not because of any Community action.

After having obtained at last the symbolic, but vital, expression of political will, albeit for a reduced effort, the Commission has concentrated on promoting three particular aspects of the New Strategy: the mobilization of alternative sources, the definition of more precise common objectives, and the definition of a common external position that was not seen as aggressive either by producers or other consumers. By this time the IEA had been formed and oil sharing arrangements agreed. The Commission recommended that the Community should take part in those oil sharing arrangements and continue to participate in the IEA. This left outstanding the knotty problem of the possible consequences of the French dissension and how to ameliorate them. For the time being, however, the Commission concentrated on trying to define common objectives.

At the meeting of Energy Ministers, the Community took a tiny step along the road to transforming the affirmation of political will into practical measures. The Council approved a resolution asking the Commission to elaborate periodically long-term guidelines for investment to achieve the objectives of the new energy strategy; the resolution was to be the basic text in the preparation of policies for the various energy sectors. The principles laid down in the resolution included:

that coal production would be maintained; this was a compromise between Germany and the United Kingdom, on the one hand, who wanted guarantees of disposal at profitable prices, and the potential users, especially France and Italy, who wanted free access to world markets;

that the Commission would draw up annually a realistic indicative programme for nuclear power and proposals for Community endeavours in procuring nuclear fuel;

that the Community would adopt joint policies for the oil industry;

that Community rules should be established for sharing oil when supplies were threatened.

The resolution was more precise than earlier agreements and as such represented progress, although painfully slow; no commitment of any substance, however, had been made, and the apparent progress could easily prove to be illusory – as indeed it was.

The Commission then shifted its efforts to the discussion of how the objectives it had indicated might be financed. It was led to do this by the frequent criticism that the financial consequences of the New Strategy would be difficult to accommodate. In June the Commission sent two memoranda to the Council.[68,69] One discussed how the Community could help directly to finance investment in her energy sources, the other discussed how the Community could create confidence in others to finance investment. The Commission asserted that the efforts being made by private enterprise and national governments should be supported by a Community effort, since the investment involved was so great that the guarantees required could only be provided satisfactorily by a body of the size and stature of the Community; it estimated that if the contribution from the Community were 15 per cent of the total, then it would have to raise 3 billion units of account each year until 1985. The financing had to be done according to a plan, which the Commission undertook to draw up each year.

In the second paper, the Commission argued that the Community should agree a policy aimed at promoting investment in energy sources other than imported oil by specific incentives, and that the investments should be safeguarded against any future fall in the price of imported oil by some form of safety net. The height of the safety net would be determined by an assessment of how much indigenous production should be protected.

With these memoranda the Commission submitted specific proposals:

for regulations relating to a common procedure for imports and exports;

to increase Community support for oil and gas prospecting;

to issue Euratom bonds as an initial Community contribution to financing nuclear power;

to take certain measures in common in the event of a supply crisis, particularly to reduce consumption and maintain trade within the Community.

The meeting was again dominated by a difference of opinion between France and the other eight member states. France was sponsoring the North-South dialogue and was unenthusiastic about measures of support or agreements on oil sharing that would effectively make her part of the IEA, or about anything that could be construed as an aggressive attitude to the oil producing countries. The other member states, although not united or enthusiastic, thought that the support measures should have priority; the United Kingdom, especially, was keen to see its investments in the North Sea protected.

The proposal for a common import and export regime for hydrocarbons was opposed by France, on the grounds that such a measure was only acceptable as part of a detailed policy of internal control. The issue of Euratom bonds did not seem to the national delegations, especially Germany, as likely to speed up programmes of nuclear power. Scepticism in this respect is lent authority by the Community's experience with the regional fund. Money from the regional fund is allocated to specific projects by the governments of the member states; as a result, the fund is used to finance projects which the national government would otherwise have financed itself. The fund replaces part of national expenditure; it does not supplement it. A somewhat similar state of affairs might well arise with Euratom loans. The Commission is fond of saying that although the funds at its disposal are small, they are effective at the margin, but because of the mechanism described above, there is actually little hard evidence that the margin is shifted at all by Community intervention.

Some improvement might result if the Commission were to allocate the regional fund to specific projects on the basis of applications made directly to it by the regional body that would spend the money; there is apparently a move to introduce this system. It is not obvious that even this arrangement will cause more money to be spent on regional development, but we cannot follow up that argument; the purpose of this digression is simply to show that it is by no means clear that Euratom bonds would speed up nuclear programmes. In the end the Council came to no decision on the general strategies for finance and protection. Nor did they agree any specific measures, but sent them all back to COREPER for further discussion.

Indeed, 1975 was another year of general resolutions and proclamations of approval; almost no decisions of substance were taken; all were returned to COREPER and groups of national experts. The anodyne exceptions were aims on the reduction of energy consumption, and directives restricting the use of petroleum and natural gas in power stations, restricting the building of or conversion to oil burning power stations, obliging member states to maintain stocks of fossil fuels at power stations, and providing some financial support for the development of indigenous hydrocarbons. The Community was, as the Commission quite rightly pointed out, just as exposed to an acute oil crisis as it had been before the Yom Kippur war.

Being due to submit an account of the progress made towards achieving the objectives for 1985, the Commission prepared to use the occasion to find out whether the member states had the political will to embark on a common energy policy worthy of the name. They therefore cast their report in the form of a questionnaire,[70] asking what measures the Community might adopt to cause member states to do certain things favourable to the Community. For example, one question concerned with North Sea oil is 'whether the implementation of suitable Community measures (what type?) would enable the United Kingdom to set itself the ambitious production target of 175 million toe [tons of oil equivalent] . . . or even higher for 1985'.

This document is very odd; it has an air of conceding all initiative with jocular despair. It was probably devised because the Energy Ministers had persistently claimed they were being asked to take decisions on matters which they had not proposed and did not necessarily think defined an appropriate approach to energy policy. The document was aimed at eliciting a more general discussion in which Ministers were likely to be more constructive.

As it happened, the Commission was pre-empted by the European Council at the Rome summit. As a formula to hide their extensive failure to agree, the European Council instructed the Commission to submit proposals for an appropriate means of:

protecting existing indigenous resources and developing alternatives;

ensuring genuine solidarity in the event of oil supply difficulties;

encouraging the rational use of energy.

That this was a formula was evident, because the Commission had already put to the Council proposals on all these matters which had neither been rejected nor accepted, but had just disappeared into the limbo of COREPER. The Commission nevertheless resubmitted their earlier proposals, along with some others.[71]

The Energy Ministers met in March 1976; nothing of substance was agreed. The proposal to encourage the development of community resources was rejected by France and Italy on the grounds that only one measure was suggested, that is the MSP, and that was not the set of balanced measures appropriate to a variety of source, especially nuclear power where the French stake is large. Germany also wanted measures to help Community coal. The proposal for arrangements for sharing in times of supply difficulties came to grief on the problem of what was the competent institution for declaring the crisis and organizing a response; eight members agreed a compromise sharing the responsibility between the Council and the Commission, but France disagreed. France was hostile in principle to many of the proposals tabled at this meeting again because they stemmed originally from initiatives in the IEA, where in February 1976 the member states had agreed in principle on an MSP of $7 per barrel, and where an oil sharing plan had been agreed over a year ago.

The Council did agree in principle a directive requiring national governments to procure details of prices for crude oil and refined products. The proposals for dealing with difficulties in supply and the questionnaire were referred to COREPER.

During the remainder of 1976 the main effort of the Commission and the member states was diverted to the North-South dialogue. The Commission did put up a paper to a meeting of Energy Ministers in October[72] to obtain a general discussion of energy policy and to establish a degree of political consensus while avoiding yet another sterile debate on specific blocked proposals. The attempt was a failure; the Ministers of France and Italy were absent and were represented by civil servants. Mr. Benn, for the United Kingdom, argued vigorously in favour of an MSP, and the meeting took precisely the form which it was hoped to avoid.

Progress in the North-South dialogue was also slow. It was expected that the conference would end sometime in mid-December with little more than a declaration of general principles. But this hope, broadly shared by the industrialized countries, was illusory, and events in the last two months were unexpectedly lively. Towards the end of November a number of members of OPEC threatened that if the final ministerial session of the North-South dialogue, scheduled for 15 December, did not satisfy their expectations, then they would respond at the OPEC meeting on 20 December with a much higher increase in oil prices. This ultimatum was clearly intended to coerce all the industrialized countries, but it was directed especially at the members of the EEC, who were due in a few days to meet at The Hague for the European Council. The oil producers and the developing countries hoped that the EEC could be persuaded to make concessions on matters such as debt relief, raw materials prices and a common commodity fund, and that the United States and Japan would be obliged to follow.

Certainly, the discussion of the North-South dialogue dominated the meeting at The Hague, although there was no shortage of other gloomy problems facing the Community. Western Europe was in grave economic circumstances; the Community in general, and the common agricultural policy and monetary policy in particular, were threatened by divergent economies; the fragile beginnings of economic recovery were threatened by another rise in oil prices. Little progress was made with any of these matters, which was understandable, but, more disappointingly, the Community appeared less unified than ever. Specifically, in the discussion of possible responses to OPEC, Germany undermined from the outset any possible Community solidarity by declaring before the conference began that she alone of Community countries could stand an oil price rise of 15 per cent, but refusing at the same time to consider concessions to developing countries; in particular, she would not tolerate the proposals for a common fund to guarantee commodity prices. Herr Schmidt proposed turning the tables on OPEC by refusing concessions within the North-South dialogue until the Community had seen the extent of the increases in the price of oil. The intentional result of this German intransigence was that the Community could not take a common position in the closing phases of the North-South dialogue. The German manoeuvres were designed to coerce the other members of the Community into adopting similar attitudes of confrontation.

Luckily for the Community the final session of the North-South dialogue was postponed early in December on the grounds that some of the countries concerned were temporarily unable to take political decisions; in the U.S.A. the new President had not yet assumed control and in Japan a new government was being formed following a general election. The reasons, although substantial, were a welcome pretext by which the industrialized countries managed an ignominious escape from the trap which they had set for themselves.

The OPEC meeting in Qatar on 20 December was preceded by a month of speculation and analysis of such factors as how the progress in the North-South dialogue would affect oil prices and how and why the price of imports to the Middle East had risen and therefore what compensating rise in oil prices was justified. But these and other such factors are just convenient fashions of providing the justification for decisions taken by OPEC essentially on the basis of four considerations:

the desire to increase revenue;

the perception of the state of Western industry and the price it would stand;

the preservation of OPEC;

the desire to influence political events.

These factors operate to different degrees in the different members. Some countries, especially Iran, which is in grave financial difficulties, are motivated almost exclusively by the first factor. Saudi Arabia, whose revenues far outweigh her financial requirements, is sufficiently relaxed about money to give considerable weight to the second and fourth factors. The desire to exert political influence is also strong in other producers, especially Libya and Algeria.

The balance of international opinion as OPEC met was that Saudi Arabia, by virtue of the large difference between its present output and its producing capacity, dominated the cartel and would keep the price low; indeed, her opening move was to propose a price freeze. After short but dramatic bargaining, OPEC finally decided on a completely unexpected two-tier price structure. Eleven members opted for an immediate 10 per cent rise in prices and a further 5 per cent from mid-1977. Saudi Arabia and the United Arab Emirates restricted their increase to 5 per cent. The decision of Saudi Arabia was conditional on progress in the North-South dialogue and, more especially, on progress towards peace in the Middle East.

On the face of it the cartel is beginning to crack and, certainly, there is no love lost between its members; Iranian representatives were furious with the decision of Saudi Arabia. But, although the two-tier price structure has brought a complex and interesting economic situation, there are many ways in which it might resolve without the cartel breaking up. The eleven members of OPEC who agreed on a 10 per cent rise might also agree to restrict their output to compensate for increased Saudi Arabian production; this does not seem likely, given the overwhelming need in some of the countries concerned for increased revenue. Saudi Arabia might choose not to expand production rapidly enough or far enough to drive the prices of her competitors down, but only enough to accommodate increases in world demand. This again is unlikely, as Saudi Arabia has already announced her intention to expand output from 8.5 million barrels a day to 10 million barrels a day and to review that level periodically. Moreover, it is unlikely for reasons of political prestige that she will be willing to concede a 10 per cent rise to her fellow producers.

The most likely development is that existing contractual agreements and investment in the militant OPEC countries will permit them to

73

maintain a price increase above 5 per cent. The price of cheap and dear crude may be equalized to an extent by the oil companies, although because of an unequal distribution of cheap and dear crude among the companies it is not clear how far the equalizing process can go. The oil companies will certainly exploit the ambiguity and take much of the difference as profit. Although the details are obscure, it is probable that the price rise to the European consumer will be nearer 10 per cent than 5 per cent.

The political consequences are far more significant. Europe was powerless to exert any influence on this decision other than by demonstrating that a large increase would damage the European economy so much as to harm the oil producers – an influence comparable to that of the goose in the tale of the golden eggs. The U.S.A. was apparently able to appease or coerce Saudi Arabia by hinting at political concessions in the Middle East. But evidently this is a substantial concession and a restriction on her independent conduct of foreign policy, which only serves to emphasize how strong are the political consequences of the oil producers' economic hold on the industrialized countries.

Finally, since 1973 a quite different, but venerable, theme of European energy policy has reappeared, which should briefly be traced – uranium enrichment. After this function had been removed from Euratom, France continued to develop techniques of enrichment by diffusion; the United Kingdom worked on enrichment by centrifugation, and Germany also investigated various methods of enrichment using centrifugal techniques. The matter became politically important again in 1972/73. The French led a consortium comprising Sweden, Italy, Belgium and Spain (EURODIF), which aimed at constructing a European plant working by diffusion. A consortium of Germany, the United Kingdom and the Netherlands (URENCO) planned to build several plants working by centrifugation. The ever stiffer contracts and prices from the AEC in Washington provided good economic justification for a European plant; for this and political reasons, the Commission and all the countries involved favoured independent European capacity.

The two systems have different technical characteristics. The diffusion system follows the usual law of economy of scale, that is, unit costs at design capacity fall with size of plant, until some new factor intervenes to restrict the scaling up of the plant. Consequently a diffusion plant needs to be of about 10,000 tonnes SWU per annum capacity in order to enjoy the full benefits of the economies of scale; this is very large in comparison to the size of the market.

The centrifuge is a rather unusual piece of process plant, in that it has a definite and distinct optimum size. This happens because output increases proportionately to the length of the rotor, whereas the material cost of the device increases as something like the square or cube of the rotor dimensions. Add to this the usual law of economies of scale and one ends up with a well-determined optimum, which is at present about 1,000 tonnes SWU per annum.

It is interesting to follow the political struggles which develop from these different technical characteristics. The diffusion system requires a large initial capital outlay; subsequently it has to be run at a high load factor. In practice, to be a respectable financial proposition such a plant requires guaranteed future sales. The EURODIF consortium planned a plant of 10,000 tonnes SWU to come into operation in 1980; to help guarantee sales France wanted European utilities to be constrained to buy in Europe. The URENCO troika was sceptical about the diffusion technology and economics. The centrifugal plants, although possibly of higher unit capital cost, can be built smaller and therefore require a smaller initial capital outlay; they are definitely cheaper to run. URENCO planned centrifuges capable of 2,000 tonnes SWU by 1980 and 10,000 tonnes SWU by 1985. It was doubtful that the European market would sustain both sets of plans. The matter was put to the Council in May 1973 and the Council prevaricated by setting up an advisory committee, COPENUR, to advise on how Europe could best cover its future needs, to what extent it should be self-sufficient, and what was the most suitable technology.

The French attempted to persuade the Commission that demand for uranium would be high enough to justify a diffusion plant. URENCO attempted to demonstrate that demand would be low and that EURODIF should not build their plant.

Subsequently European utilities placed orders with American organizations rather than EURODIF or URENCO; this was particularly bad news for EURODIF, which depended on a massive market. But then the oil crisis gave rise to extensive new plans for nuclear plant, and for a time adequate markets were expected for both consortia. EURODIF now claims to have guaranteed sales for its output and such severe default conditions that the economic success of the plant is assured. However, it is essentially linked to the massive French nuclear programme, which is itself of dubious economic merit; if French utilities pay for defaulting the enrichment programme cannot be said to be sound, even though, technically, its revenue is unaffected.

Although each technology has its partisans who detect a significant economic advantage, it is probable that the economic performances of each technology in suitable conditions differ less than uncertainties in the appraisal. The conditions, however, are important. The extent to which Europe will be allowed to enrich uranium by the producing countries and even the amount of enrichment Europe will require in the future are so uncertain that the extra flexibility of the centrifugal technology makes it most suitable for European needs. The small sizes and short lead-times permit capacity to be built when it is fairly clear that it will be required, and in the amounts required. Nevertheless, since the oil crisis the question of enrichment has fallen a little back from the front rank.

F. Review

In general, energy policy since 1968 has followed a disheartening pattern. The Council of Ministers or the European Council affirms its political resolve and instructs the Commission to prepare proposals. After long delay the proposals are considered by the Council, which is unable to take a view, and the proposals are referred to COREPER. Subsequently a fresh affirmation of political resolve resurrects the procedure. The amount agreed is small compared to the amount of activity, and difficult for the reader to retain. The Council has so far approved:

general objectives for 1985 which commit no one;

objectives for reducing the consumption of energy whose success can never be verified;

target reduction in oil consumption;

a basic information system;

an obligation to maintain 90 days stocks of oil;

an obligation to maintain stocks of fuel at power stations;

a directive restricting the building of or conversion to oil-burning power stations;

an agreement in principle that national governments should be responsible for procuring details of prices for crude oil and products, as they are imported and as they leave the refinery;

directives restricting the use of natural gas and petroleum in power stations;

some financial support, that is, financing of Community projects for developing hydrocarbon resources and research;

some specific, but very weak, directives on the rational use of energy.

An account of the secondary legislation of the EEC in energy policy is given in Appendix II.

At the time of writing (December 1976) the objectives of the 1985 policy are in a shambles; there is no sign of a more effective effort being made, and the member states have dug themselves into positions of little or no strategic significance in relation to the questions at issue. The saddest illustration of this was the most recent Council of the Energy Ministers on 21 December, held as the OPEC countries were meeting. The United Kingdom reiterated its commitment to an MSP for oil, France refused any such concession, and in retaliation the United

Kingdom indicated that it would block the scheme for Euratom loans favoured by France. It is doubtful if either of these proposals is of practical significance, and to see two principal members of the Community locked in this futile struggle is depressing.

As for the 1985 objectives, despite the substantial quantities of oil that will soon come from the North Sea the Community's dependence on imported oil is increasing. By 1985, on present trends, the member states will import 20 per cent more oil than in 1976. The consumption of energy fell in 1974 and 1975; it was difficult to be sure which of many contenders was the principal cause. But consumption in 1976 was higher than in 1975, and it now seems likely that the fall was a result mainly of the recession, only indirectly of higher prices, and hardly at all of any sustained effort at conservation. The nuclear capacity now planned by member states is 125 GW out of 220 GW proposed by the Commission; 35 GW of the present estimate depend on decisions which have yet to be confirmed, and which more likely than not will be postponed.

The United Kingdom is firmly of the belief that she was cheated of an MSP in Rome and has made the unnecessary quest for a floor price into a matter of national honour. She has offended all her partners by making it a condition for the award of drilling licences in the North Sea that all oil be landed in the United Kingdom, in breach of EEC regulations on competition. The lines of battle have been drawn up and there is little immediate prospect of compromise.

In the meantime the problem has not gone away. The North-South dialogue has failed, unsurprisingly, to reach any agreement on a fair distribution of the world's wealth. It has become a political weapon with which the oil producers can beat the industrialized countries, or, less picturesquely, it provides a convenient political justification for shrewd commercial policies. The Community is just as vulnerable to the oil producers as it was three years ago. The only difference is that the oil producers now appreciate that they are near the point of diminishing returns and that price rises in percentage terms must be restricted, but the effect of these smaller rises on the Community may still be just as serious as the enormous increases made earlier from a much lower base.

The Euro-Arab dialogue, the International Energy Agency and the North-South dialogue, which have absorbed much of the effort of the Directorate General for Energy and much of the time the Commission has to spare for energy, may or may not have been fruitful in their own way. They have, however, distracted from the creation of a common energy policy. The Community has not agreed enough within itself to define a common attitude to energy policy; consequently the Community presence at international conferences and its participation in international agreements can only be a charade; the Community represents no point of view.

This is not to say that European nations cannot influence to some extent the international environment in which they frame their energy policies; nor that a Community energy policy is necessary if European nations are to influence events; but if European interests are to be represented by the Community, then it is necessary that they agree sufficiently to make this representation effective.

One official of the Community, when asked why the 'energy crisis' had not stimulated progress on the common energy policy, replied that it was because eight member states had chosen to seek American support rather than to support themselves. The decline of common action is reinforced by a continuous cycle; emphasis on an external policy detracts from the search for accord on a common internal policy, absence of a common internal policy makes the Community ineffective outside. Similarly, in the Euro-Arab Dialogue; it is undoubtedly true that there is a special relationship between Europe and the Middle East; the history of United Kingdom and French diplomacy in the Middle East has been chequered, but wise or foolish the presence has always been strong and a residue remains. Of more substance, the Middle East is the largest exporter of oil in the world and is economically dependent upon trade of that commodity; Europe is the world's largest importer of oil and equally dependent on that trade. Of all the main oil importing areas, Europe is also the nearest to the Middle East. Whether one likes it nor not a special relationship exists – *de facto*. It can be argued with conviction that the expectations of individual European nations from this special relationship differ so much that no common approach is conceivable, since the expectations of countries like the United Kingdom owning high-cost oil are evidently different from those of a country like France. That may well be, but if any common approach is to be made, then it can only have come significance if the Community has first agreed how to balance its internal differences in expectations and aims. A common European policy will not evolve in the course of a dialogue with Middle Eastern countries.

It is not difficult to agree with the French on the general principle that if the Community is to be an effective participant in international affairs, then the member states must first consent to a common policy.

References

1. The declaration of 9 May 1950 by Robert Schuman, then French Minister for Foreign Affairs, speaking on behalf of the government.
2. W. G. Jensen, *Energy in Europe, 1945–1980* (G. T. Foulis, London, 1967).
3. Nigel Despicht, 'Transport,' in *Europe Tomorrow*, ed. Richard Mayne (Chatham House: PEP, 1972).
4. Peter R. Odell, *Oil and World Power* (Pelican, 1970).
5. T. Rifari, *The Pricing of Crude Oil* (Praeger, 1974).

6. *The Price of Oil in Western Europe* (United Nations, Geneva, March 1955).
7. Jean Monnet, *Les Echos*, special end-of-year issue, 1955.
8. *Keesing's Contemporary Archives*, 11–18 August 1956.
9. *Resolution of the Foreign Ministers of the European Coal and Steel Community at the Messina Conference, 2 June 1955, Cmnd 9525* (HMSO, London, 1955). See also *Keesing's Contemporary Archives*, 11–18 August 1956.
10. J. G. Polack, *Euratom* (Oceana Publications, New York, 1964).
11. *Rapport des Chefs de Délégation aux Ministres des Affaires Etrangères* (Comité Intergouvernemental Créé par la Conférence de Messine, Bruxelles, 21 avril 1956).
12. Foreword to reference 11. This and other extracts from reference 11 are free translations by the author.
13. It is interesting to trace this sense of urgency in a later speech by M. Spaak to the Common Assembly of the ECSC, in which he compared the state of Europe not only the U.S.A. but to the Communist countries, who had launched a 'colossal challenge to the economies of the Western world – a challenge to which no single Western European country could hope to reply'; in this connection he quoted reports that the U.S.S.R. was training a million atomic technicians and claimed that separately the European states could never catch up.
14. E.g. Dennis Swann, *The Economics of the Common Market* (Penguin, 1975).
15. Louis Armand, *Quelques aspects du problème européen de l'Energie* (OEEC, Paris, July 1955).
16. Louis Armand, Franz Etzel and Franceso Giordani, *Target for Euratom* (May 1957).
17. *L'Europe face à ses besoins croissants en Energie* (OEEC, Paris, May 1956).
18. *Oil – the outlook for Europe* (OEEC, Paris, September 1956).
19. Henri Rieben, Euratom, nécessité vitale et urgente pour la France et pour l'Europe, *Revue Economique et Sociale* (Lausanne, January 1957).
20. Communiqué reproduced in full in reference 19.
21. *Implications and lessons of the Suez crisis* (OEEC, Paris, January 1958).
22. These figures are the forecasts for 1975 of the Harley report (reference 17) recalculated from better statistics of present consumption and more modern conventions for expressing energy as a common unit; they are given in *Towards a new energy pattern in Europe* (OEEC, January 1960).
23. Figures are the central estimate of *Target for Euratom* (reference 16); some other estimates in the *Target* were more optimistic about indigenous coal.
24. Taken from *Report on the Achievement of the Community energy policy objectives for 1985*, Com(76)9 (Brussels, January 1976).
25. *Keesing's Contemporary Archives*, 13–20 October 1956.
26. For evidence of the extent to which thermonuclear weapons were a prime objective of many French politicians, see Bernard Goldschmidt, *Les Rivalités Atomiques, 1939–1966* (Fayard, 1967).
27. W. G. Jensen, *Nuclear Power* (G. T. Foulis, London, 1967).

28. *Protocole sur les moyens d'assurer une politique coordonnée dans le domaine de l'énergie* (574/57, J.O., 7 December 1957).
29. *Etude sur la structure et les tendances de l'économie énergétique dans les pays de la Communauté: Etudes et documents* (CECA, Comité Mixte, Conseil des Ministres – Haute Authorité, 1957).
30. For reference a list of the principal dates in the progress of European integration and the changing perception of energy supplies to Europe is given in Appendix I (page 165).
31. *13th General Report of the ECSC* (1965).
32. *5th General Report of the ECSC* (1957).
33. P. H. Frankel, *Matter: Oil and Power Politics* (Faber, London, 1966).
34. *8th General Report of the ECSC* (1960).
35. *9th General Report of the ECSC* (1961).
36. *Memorandum sur la politique énergétique, 25 June 1962* (ECSC, Luxembourg, August 1962).
37. *Etudes sur les perspectives énergétiques à long terme de la Communauté Européenne* (Luxembourg, December 1962). Reference basis for 36, published later.
38. *5th General Report EAEC* (1962). Sections 228–229.
39. *5th General Report EEC* (1962). Sections 92–99.
40. *10th General Report ECSC* (1962). Sections 81–100.
41. *6th General Report EEC* (1963). Sections 112–118.
42. *11th General Report ECSC* (1963). Sections 196–237.
43. *Action Programme of the Community for the Second Stage* (Commission of the European Communities, Brussels, October 1962).
44. 'Protocole d'accord relatif aux problèmes énergétiques', *Journal officiel des Communautés Européennes*, 30 April 1964.
45. *13th General Report of the ECSC* (1965). Sections 64–101.
46. *Memorandum on the Coal Production Target for 1970 and on Coal Policy*; see *15th General Report ECSC* (1967). Sections 89–91.
47. *First illustrative Programme for the European Atomic Energy Community* (EAEC, Brussels, 1966).
48. *Première orientation pour une politique énergétique communautaire*. Commission of the European Communities, Brussels, 1968).
49. *Fuel Policy, Cmd 3438* (HMSO, London, 1967).
50. *Progrès nécessaires de la politique énergétique communautaire, Com(72)1200* (Brussels, 1972).
51. *Les problèmes et les moyens de la politique de l'énergie pour la période 1975–1985, Com(72)1201* (Brussels, 1972).
52. *Guidelines and Priority Activities under the Community Energy Policy, SEC(73) 1481* (April 1973).
53. *7th General Report, ECSC, EEC, EAEC* (Brussels, 1973).
54. Quoted in *The Economist*, 26 May 1973, p. 58.
55. *Problems in the Energy Sector, Com(74)20* (Brussels, January 1974).
56. *Measures to be adopted in consequence of the present energy crisis in the Community, Com(74)40* (Brussels, January 1974).
57. *Towards a new energy policy for the European Community* (*Bulletin of the European Communities, Supplement 4/74*, Brussels, 1974).

58. *ibid* page 7, author's italics.
59. *ibid* page 7.
60. *Community energy policy objectives for 1985, Com(74)1960* (Brussels, 1974),
61. *Medium term guidelines for the electricity sector, Com(74)1970* (Brussels, 1974).
62. *Towards a Community nuclear fuel supply policy, Com(74)1963* (Brussels, 1974).
63. *Medium term guidelines for coal 1975–1985, Com(74)1860* (Brussels, 1974).
64. *Community policy in the hydrocarbon sector, Com(74)1961* (Brussels, 1974).
65. *Support to common projects for hydrocarbon exploration, Com(74)1962* (Brussels, 1974).
66. *Measures to be taken in the event of oil supply difficulties, Com(74)1964* (Brussels, 1974).
67. *Community action programmes and draft Council resolution on the rational utilisation of energy, Com(74)1950* (Brussels, 1974).
68. *Community financing of energy policy* (Brussels, 1975).
69. *Main foci of a policy for the development of energy resources in the Community and within the Larger Framework of International Cooperation, Com(75)310* (Brussels, 1975).
70. *Report on the achievement of the Community energy policy objectives for 1985 Com(76)9* (Brussels, 1976).
71. *Implementation of the Energy Policy Guidelines, Com(75)691* (Brussels, 1976).
72. *Community Energy Policy, Com(76)508* (Brussels, 1976).

II

Procedure for Making Policy

A. The Dialogue between Council and Commission

The formal procedure by which decisions are made within the Community has been described many times.[1,2,3] In the original theory the most important element was the relationship between the sovereign states and the executive of the Community; for the enterprise to succeed it was recognized that the executive must have some power to balance the sovereignty of the member states. In the ECSC Treaty the High Authority was given specific powers over the economies of member states and was assigned the responsibility for implementing the Treaty; the consent of the Council, in some cases a unanimous consent, is only necessary in certain important matters. At the time when the EEC and Euratom were formed it was unlikely that the member states would have again consented to assign similar supranational powers to the executive; moreover, it was not an appropriate way of giving the executive authority in fields where no clear agreement was yet foreseen or had yet been attempted. More subtle means were used. It was arranged that the Council could only debate matters on which proposals had been submitted by the executive – the Commission therefore had the power of initiative in policy. Moreover, the Council could only amend a proposal of the Commission by a unanimous vote; a majority of the Council is therefore not enough to direct policy without the consent of the Commission. After the merger of the Executives in 1967 the relationship between the Commission and the Council under the Treaty of Paris and the Treaties of Rome still retained this essential difference. Basically, under the Treaty of Paris the Commission decides with the Council's endorsement; under the Treaties of Rome the Council decides on the Commission's proposal. The procedure in the Rome Treaty is the most common. Either way, if the Commission does not propose then no progress is possible, and this is meant to ensure that the Commission has some real bargaining power in the dialogue with the Council. The mechanism was conceived as the truly original feature of the Community institutions. The initiative of the Commission, the response of the Council and the synthesis by the Commission was seen as a dialectic that would be the motive force of the Community.

It is difficult to know how well this theory has stood the test of time. Matters are evidently in practice much more complicated. The Committee of Permanent Representatives (COREPER) is frequently identified nowadays as being the body in which the bulk of arbitration on political matters takes place. The European Councils also evidently exert erratic but important influence. But the formal mechanism of the dialogue between the Commission and the Council is still a useful point from which to begin an account of the decision-making process.

B. Consultation of Outside Bodies by the Commission

1. THE IMPORTANCE OF CONSULTATION TO THE COMMISSION

Consultation of outside bodies is absolutely essential to the successful performance of the functions of the Commission. There are three main reasons for this: the weak technical base of the Commission, the eventual need to obtain the consent of member states to proposals, and the Commission's permanent need for information. The limit to the technical work that the Commission can do is quickly reached. The Directorate-General of Energy has about 30 staff of graduate status, far less than an analogous Department of State in a national administration. Some of them are technical men whose knowledge is dated, some of them are economists or lawyers without specific technical training. It is necessary to get technologists from outside to participate, and to do this requires first of all a political impulse to stimulate the awareness of the problem, so that national governments will encourage their staff to participate in expert committees and will agree to send along competent representatives whose absence from other affairs is a perceptible loss. The second step, in principle, is to capture the imagination of the technologists participating in expert committees so that they will feel committed to some extent to the objectives of the Community. Judging by interviews with national representatives on the advisory committees for energy and for research and development related to energy, the second step is rarely made; the imagination of outsiders is rarely captured, and they are more likely to see themselves as providing a formal show of consultation with little chance of altering the intentions of Commission officials.

Many of the meetings of experts are arranged for particular matters as they arise; others have been made, by one means or another, permanent institutions. In energy matters some of the committees that might be consulted are: the ECSC Consultative Committee, which was set up by the Treaty of Paris and contains representatives of trade associations, trade unions and coal users; the Committee for Research in Energy Related Science and Technology (CREST); the Steering Committee for the Rational Use of Energy; the Permanent Committee on the Enrichment of Uranium (COPENUR); and the Nuclear Research Advisory Committee. Meetings are also held with pressure groups of various sorts; in energy matters this would include the trade associations of electricity producers and distributors (UNIPEDE), coal producers (CEPCEO), and oil companies. These pressure groups exist to prosecute the interests of their members, but in doing so they are a source of information and technical expertise to the Commission.

The need eventually to obtain the consent of member governments to proposals also justifies extensive consultation. It is important if the Commission's proposals are to succeed that they should be not only technically sound, but also politically acceptable to member governments. Evidently the officials of the Commission will pick up an impression of what is politically acceptable from a wide variety of sources. At one extreme the officials have access to the accounts of the mass media, as does any citizen, and at the other extreme they can, in the Council of Ministers, observe at first hand the preoccupations of national governments. However, a great deal of their comprehension of the political constraints which operate in member states will come during consultation with COREPER and other similar groups of national representatives, for example the Energy Committee and the High-Level Working Group on Energy. The function of these bodies will be discussed in more detail later.

The Commission's continual thirst for information can also be partly satisfied by consultation. The Commission needs to be well informed about national policies, intentions in investment, existing investment, problems and expectations if it is to act constructively. For a long time in energy matters the Commission did not have access by right to even the most basic factual information. A series of directives has now changed that situation, but the Commission still needs to know about intentions and expectations which are not firm enough to be supplied to it officially or which fall outside the scope of the existing directives. To supply this information consultation at all levels is helpful.

2. THE EXTENT AND NATURE OF CONSULTATION

The extent to which the Commission consults outside bodies before framing its policies depends on many factors and one can only generalize tentatively. With this caveat, it is possible to distinguish different approaches according to whether the Commission is trying to establish the broad lines of a policy in a new area and to extract from the Council a political stimulus, or whether the Commission is trying to devise difficult measures for the execution of an established policy.

When the Commission proposes a particular measure which, if adopted, will cause perceptible changes in the conduct of affairs in member states It anticipates keen bargaining, detailed examination and frequent modification to meet conflicting interests as far as possible. The Commission wishes the chance of the proposal being accepted to be as high as possible; it therefore tries by extensive preliminary consultation within committees of national civil servants to arrive at a formula which is as acceptable as possible whilst being consistent with the objectives of the Commission.

An example of this sort of consultative procedure is the Commission's work on the safety of nuclear power stations. The prerogative of decisions on the siting, construction and operation of nuclear power stations has always lain with member states; the Euratom Treaty did not foresee a Community licensing agency, but the Commission as a focus of consultation and a stimulus to harmonization has been working on the matter since 1959. Licensing decisions are made in member states by a variety of authorities, according to widely varying procedures,[4] but the decision in all cases is based on a detailed technical assessment of reactor and site. The Commission's contribution was to bring together technical experts from the member states to express an opinion on a project should a national administration ask the Commission for technical advice. In the course of this function the Commission produced a number of safety reports; although these had nothing more than the status of advice, they helped harmonization of standards indirectly by facilitating exchange of information and encouraging the common choice of the most satisfactory procedures. This is an example of an activity in which the Commission has initiated a consultative procedure not even for the purpose of making specific proposals, but simply for the indirect benefit of information, prestige and technical understanding.

The closely related matter of nuclear safety provides an example of consultative procedures leading to specific proposals. The Commission considered that there were sound economic and political reasons to try to harmonize safety practices in the nuclear industry and co-ordinate research into nuclear safety. It set up several working groups to discuss the matter with expert representatives of licensing authorities, utilities, manufacturers and national civil servants. After painstaking progress the consultative procedure culminated in a report and a draft resolution to the Council. The resolution on technological problems of nuclear safety was adopted by the Council in July 1975. It called on member states to improve their collaboration on safety matters with the eventual aim of adopting similar safety practices and criteria. As a result of the Council resolution the Commission then felt able to submit two proposals[5,6] to strengthen the secretariat of the working parties of national experts. The proposals have not yet been accepted. The example is not dramatic, but it has been chosen to show how extensive is discussion and how progress may only be made, if it is made at all, by tiny steps.

When formulating the main lines of policy the Commission is relatively free to set out its own position based on the information and opinion of its own departments, although in practice, even at this stage, its statements may be modified by what it believes to be acceptable to member states. In this situation the Commission will first undertake preliminary consultations with national politicians and civil servants, industrialists and unions, and then will go ahead and produce its own opinion. The reasoning in support of this procedure is that the Commission has no national interest; it is the guardian of the Community interest and responsible only to the European Parliament; its duty is to produce a European policy; too much attention to national special pleading in the first instance would distract from this duty. So, for example, if the Commission were considering a new initiative in coal policy it would start with informal soundings of national governments, coal producers and electricity producers in order to get the feel of things. The Commission would then put forward its own views in a working document which would contain one or more formulations of the aims of the initiative and a choice of procedures. The working document would then be discussed with interested organizations on a more formal basis, for example the ECSC Consultative Committee, UNIPEDE for electricity producers, CEPCEO for coal producers, and national civil servants within the various groups (COREPER, the Working Groups on Energy and the Energy Committee). This is probably the point in the procedure where the bulk of arbitration on technical matters occurs and where the Commission learns most. Of course, the information is invariably put across with a more or less overt political aim – for example, in the ECSC Consultative Committee the presence of coal mining management and labour demands that appropriate attitudes be struck.

The working document will normally go through several drafts and the Commission may revise its ideas; interaction with the world outside may become less technical and more political, with an increasing emphasis on consultation with national administrations from whom consent is finally to be sought. Eventually the Commission will decide on proposals and submit them formally to the Council of Ministers.

The grand strategies extending over the whole of energy policy are produced in a similar way, although the extent of consultation varies enormously. On occasions it may be extensive, as appears to have been the case with the *First Guidelines towards a Community Energy Policy*.[7] In this instance the Commission needed to acquire a lot of information from member governments before being able to produce the solid basis they wanted for a common policy; this was a long business, so long that in the end the political momentum was lost before the policy appeared. Such extensive consultation at the stage of broad strategies is probably the exception. More typical was the *New Energy Strategy*[8] which was produced after little consultation; even when member states were consulted the Commission mostly went ahead with its own ideas.

C. Consultation within the Commission

In all its decisions the Commission acts as a collegiate body, and it cannot in principle delegate powers to individuals in any but the most restricted technical sphere. In principle, therefore, proposals put forward by the Commission for a common energy policy are supported by all Commissioners. This does not mean that they all necessarily agree with the proposals, but the minority always abides by the majority decision which subsequently becomes the opinion of the entire Commission. In matters of energy policy the Commissioner for Energy is naturally influential; the Commissioners for External Relations, Industry, Transport (because of the transport of nuclear fuels), Social Affairs (because of the effects of radioactive emissions), Research, Environment and the Euratom Supply Agency would have a direct interest; the other Commissioners might or might not have a strong interest depending on their personal priorities, but they have no *locus standi* and probably little influence; the President of the Commission inevitably is much involved because he carries the responsibility for achieving an acceptable consensus within the Commission.

The Cabinet system of the Commission also influences the nature of consensus. Each Commissioner has a private office or Cabinet of people, usually of his own nationality, to advise him. These advisers have, like the Commissioner, essentially political functions and experience. Several members of this office may specialize in aspects of the Commissioner's own portfolio and develop profound technical knowledge. Others may cover several policy areas outside the Commissioner's immediate interests. Simply because of the limits on human ability their technical knowledge must be limited, but communication between the Cabinets is efficient, far better than between members of a Cabinet and the staff of a different Directorate-General, or, indeed, between the staffs of different Directorate-Generals. Information on a matter outside his own competence will therefore come to a Commissioner by means of two Cabinets; the presentation will inevitably be highly political. The chances of a Commissioner being able to gather support for a measure among his colleagues on mainly political grounds and in conflict with technical considerations are amplified by the Cabinet system.

There is no apparent evidence of any appreciable dissension within the Commission over the New Energy Strategy, although it has been claimed that some of the proposals which arose out of that strategy have been the cause of dissent, especially the proposal for a minimum support price for oil. Even the initial draft with objectives for 1985 of 220 GW(e) of nuclear capacity and a 40 per cent dependence on imports did not strain the doctrine of collegiate responsibility.

In a way this is surprising because there appears to have been substantial dissension amongst the officers of the Commission's own departments. In the course of interviews with officials in late 1975 and early 1976 it was difficult to find anyone willing to defend the substance of the ambitious targets of the New Energy Strategy even within the Directorate-General for Energy. A persistently reiterated belief maintains that the energy policy strategy was almost exclusively the intellectual property of the past Director-General for Energy and a small group of advisers; the efforts of the majority of staff in the Directorate-General were directed to justifying such performances within their particular energy sector as would best fit the preconceived strategy. The strategy did have consequences for other Directorate-Generals. The ability, or otherwise, of the Community industries to manufacture the components and construct plant would be a matter for the Directorate-General for Industry. The safety of workers and the public, the finding of sites, the training of operators and the management of waste are all matters which, although for all practical purposes are the responsibility of national administrations, are watched over for the Commission by the Directorate-General for Industry. Interviews with officials in this Directorate-General revealed varying degrees of concern with these consequences. If one could distinguish a general attitude it would probably be that the Community could indeed mount an effort of this magnitude in terms of manufacturing equipment and constructing plants.[9] But the implications in terms of siting and safety, the necessity to obtain public support, the quality control of manufacture, construction and operation, and the disposal of waste are sufficient to make the proposals unrealistic. All these problems, and even the possibility of a serious accident, are exacerbated if nuclear power is promoted without proper control and environmental care, as would happen with the rapid rates of development proposed.

These consequences, though, are not of immediate importance to the Directorate-General for Energy because their responsibilities do not extend to these matters.

Not surprisingly perhaps, opinion in the Environment and Consumer Protection Service also contains some criticism of the energy policy strategy. Here it is felt that the basis of the projections of energy demand have never been seriously questioned; little attention has been paid to how the structure of energy use may evolve and how that may modify demand; inadequate consideration has been given to the en vironmental consequences and the constraints of public opinion.

No doubt similar criticisms could be found in other Directorate-Generals with a direct interest in energy policy. It would appear that the implications of the strategy were put to the Commission, but not pressed. If this is true, one is tempted to conclude that in the formulation of general strategies for policy the Commissioner and Directorate-General most immediately concerned have almost a free hand and that it is only when policy has developed to the stage where proposals of practical effect are mooted that the collegiate responsibility of the Commission comes under stress.

Whether or not the reservations about the nuclear proposals evident in the Directorate-General for Industry and elsewhere among officials were expressed within the Commission itself, it is clear that, although the Commission acting as a collegiate body may give unanimous support to the new strategy, there can conceivably still be dissension among the officials.

Consultation between services does not appear to be commensurate with the division of responsibility for the various aspects of energy policy. This assertion receives some support from conversations with officials; it is said that interservice groups are often ineffective and rarely set up until after proposals have been finalized; transmission of information is largely vertical. Poor co-ordination in energy policy is likely to be particularly serious where many interests are involved coming under different departments. The most extreme example is, of course, in nuclear matters which, after the merger of the Commissions, were absorbed into several different departments. In this instance a permanent nuclear co-ordination group has been set up at *Chef de Cabinet* level to work out a Commission policy which is largely agreed by all services. It is still said that co-ordination between departments is inadequate and the past performance of the Commission on energy policy does not refute those allegations.

The relationship between the Commissioner and his department, particularly his Director-General, may take a variety of forms and may influence the nature and success of policy. One can only speculate, but there are two generalizations which may be valid. Firstly, the Cabinet system gives the Commissioner a strong base if he wishes to go against his department; secondly, the more technical the subject the more the balance tilts to the Director-General.

A Commissioner can build up a strong Cabinet and provide himself with an alternative source of advice to his department. What the Cabinet lacks in technical background may be compensated by good lines of communication with other Cabinets and more political astuteness than the officers of the department. Conflict between a Commissioner and his Director-General is not unknown in the Commission; it has happened, for example, with pragmatic Director-Generals of the United Kingdom civil service tradition and the more flamboyant continental Commissioners of the federalist persuasion. When there is conflict the effectiveness of the department is inevitably reduced; the outcome will be decided by a variety of factors, but to some extent in highly technical affairs the advantage will shift towards the Director-General because of the necessity in such cases for sound technical information and advice, and because in practice there are many powerful interests external to the Commission, for example state industries and oil companies, whose acquiescence in an energy policy is very nearly essential and with whom, by the nature of the system, the Directorate-General will have more effective relations than the Cabinet.

D. Presentation and Mediation of National Interests

In the simple theory the Commission interacts directly with the Council; in practice this was more or less true for the ECSC, but for the EEC and EAEC the Council was assisted by a Committee of Permanent Representatives (COREPER) comprising permanent representatives of the member states to the Communities. Initially the role of the Committee was not codified, but the merger treaty confirmed its existence and its responsibility for preparing the material for discussion in the Council. The significance of COREPER is still in many ways obscure and a subject of disagreement between the most eminent authorities in European institutions; here we can do no more than note the divergences of opinion where appropriate.

The Council of Ministers is a bad decision-making body if only because of the chaos in which meetings are held. Each government normally sends one minister, but he is accompanied by many advisers and the total of all the delegation may be enormous; the Commission is also present in force. In these circumstances no negotiation is possible. The Council meetings certainly do serve to make the political pressures bearing on the political representatives of the member states clear to the permanent representatives of the other members and also to the Commission, but the Council can really only say yes or no, or refer the matter back to COREPER. It is clear from the history of EEC energy policy in the preceding chapter that the ministers responsible for energy have been especially limited in their response to Council proposals. On a few occasions the Council has modified a proposal, but only towards greater conservatism, as for example its revision of the targets for 1985 back down to the sum of national programmes, and even here the compromise had been discussed and tentatively agreed in COREPER beforehand.

The role of COREPER is to go over the preliminary ground and establish areas of disagreement On less important matters where COREPER and the Commission agree the decision can be made to all intents and purposes by COREPER; on more important matters and on all matters with political implications the proposals will be passed to the Council of Ministers. The Council is unlikely in practice to make any decision, but its discussion will expose the political preoccupations of the member states and allow the permanent representatives to cite these as constraints in later sessions. A controversial proposal will in all likelihood be referred back to COREPER. This second time round the Committee may attempt to bargain; it will work with the Commission, and in principle the beginnings of a compromise solution could emerge, reflecting the constraints of domestic politics in member states.

The force of the procedure for producing a European solution to questions, rather than the solution which offends member states the least, has been weakened since the early 1960s. In the field of energy, a resurgence of nationalism both in France and Germany, combined with conflicting interests in the protection of the European coal industry, had put great strain on the common policy. Although this was papered over by the *Protocol d'Accord* in 1964, the Commission was made well aware that it could no longer expect member states to adopt proposals affecting their economies with which they did not fully agree. Of even more general significance within the Community was the French walk-out in 1965, ostensibly to express dislike of Commission proposals to tie completion of the regulations for financing the agricultural policy, which were strongly desired by France, to other measures of which France disapproved. The protest was also directed obliquely, but plainly enough in the Community world, at the system of qualified majority voting to be introduced in 1966. The consequence was the Luxembourg compromise of January 1966 which required that in matters of vital national interest, which has come to mean all and everything, a unanimous decision of the Council be obtained.

To avoid a repetition of all this the Commission no longer pushes its proposals so hard; it probably also makes less effort to get the vigorous support of a particular nation, because in the long run a consensus will be necessary. The Commission now prefers to confine disputes to the secrecy of COREPER rather than to let them emerge publicly in the Council of Ministers; the mediative function of COREPER therefore grows in importance.

The member states are equally agreeable to this transfer of arbitration and negotiation to COREPER. As the matters which European unity began to affect grew proportionately more important to member states, so they attempted to withdraw these matters from the Commission and have them dealt with by institutions with a clear nationalist representation; the larger the issue in the European Community the more pronounced is this tendency. The governments of member states, being much more given to secrecy than the European Commission, have evidently also an interest in keeping matters hidden in COREPER. Consequently both member states and the Commission have colluded in transferring the greatest part of arbitration on European affairs into COREPER and other international, rather than supranational, institutions.

Throughout the preceding discussion the title COREPER has stood for a variety of intergovernmental institutions which are not strictly part of COREPER, although they have a similar function. There is evidence that at least in energy policy the greatest part of negotiation and arbitration takes place not in COREPER itself, but in specialized committees. It is important, therefore, to examine more closely the structure of the array of intergovernmental institutions. For proposals relating to energy the critical institution is the Council Working Group on Energy. This comprises national civil servants and people from the Commission, that is administrators not Commissioners. This Working Group meets at two levels, roughly at the level of principals and assistant-secretaries and at a higher level up to the Director-General from the Commission and Permanent Secretaries or their national equivalents from the member states. The United Kingdom representatives come from the Department of Energy and also from the Permanent Representatives in Brussels.

The Commission's proposals go first to COREPER and are discussed briefly, some guidelines of a slightly political character may be suggested and areas of disagreement defined. The proposals then go to the Working Group on Energy who take the discussion as far as they can. The dossier then goes back to COREPER, often only shortly before the meeting of the Council of Ministers. Where there is basic disagreement at the level of the Working Group it is difficult for COREPER to do anything. Consequently, obtaining agreement in the High-Level Working Group is the most crucial step in getting proposals accepted.

One result of the Copenhagen summit in December 1973 in the aftermath of the oil crisis was to establish an Energy Committee of the European Communities. This is a Council body comprising senior officials from the member states, but it is chaired by the Commission, often indeed by the Commissioner. It was set up to help the Commission frame proposals which stood a chance of being acceptable to member states; the Energy Committee would be available for consultation before sending proposals to the Council; it was a formal sounding board extending the Commission's means of informal reconnaissance.

The jobs of the Energy Committee and the High-Level Working Group are in principle different, but there does in practice seem to have been a struggle between the two for influence. The High-Level Working Group is thought to be winning, in part because of the way the Energy Committee has been used by the Commission, which in turn is partly a result of the (changing) tradition of rather restricted consultation of national governments before proposals are first made. The Council has tried to use the Energy Committee as a way of putting the brake on the Commission's ambitious energy proposals, the Commission has tried to use the Committee as a way of lending their proposals authority by a show of prior consultation, and not surprisingly it does not have an influence commensurate with the status of its members.

Another potential forum for negotiation and another potential source of initiative is the meeting of the Heads of State in the European Council or summit conferences. The decision to hold regular meetings of Heads of States was no doubt partly prompted by the desire of member states to keep a firm grip on some of the increasingly important topics that were being included in the expanding sphere of influence of the Community, but also partly by the recognition that the Council-Commission dialectic was failing to provide the driving force for the Community. The general diagnosis popular at the time was that the Community suffered from a lack of political will; the cause having a highly political content, it was reasonable to prescribe a high political institution for the cure.

The European Council has several times declared its political will to form a common energy policy or called on the Commission to submit proposals to that end; this happened notably at the Paris summit in October 1972, the Copenhagen summit in December 1973 and the Rome summit in December 1975. The results are thin. In contrast, the European Council does succeed in certain instances when dealing with high political matters of no great technical complexity and where the decision to be made is simple in form. The Copenhagen summit in December 1973 managed to preserve a semblance of political unity in trying conditions, and recently the Council agreed to proceed with direct elections to the European Parliament. Even if the constant calls from the summit for a common energy policy were genuine and not a formula to disguise the lack of ideas and agreement it is unlikely that they would have any success, because the Council in a matter of much technical complexity cannot itself produce a satisfactory policy. This can only be done by the Commission and the intergovernmental committees of national civil servants. It is doubtful if these expert committees have incentive enough to agree a common policy or common measures in the energy sector in the face of the genuine and difficult obstacles.

Once European integration ceased to comprise adjustments of technical matters and common regulations of affairs, it was inevitable that the intergovernmental institutions would encroach on the supranational institutions. COREPER served to mediate between member states in an intergovernmental environment, in which function it was encroaching on the prerogative of the Commission. The European Council further eroded the influence and authority of the Commission by transferring to itself considerable powers of initiative, to define areas in which proposals should be elaborated and to sketch the form proposals should take, and considerable powers to make decisions, albeit only in broad terms because of practical limits to the amount of detail that can be dealt with at this highest level.

There is controversy as to whether the COREPER, the European Council and similar intergovernmental institutions divide the dialogue between the Commission and the Council or develop it more effectively. Equally eminent authorities with long experience in Community institutions disagree. M. Emile Noël[10] argues that from living and working in the environment of the Commission the Permanent Representatives absorb European ideals and convert the wilfulness of national politicians to potential compromise. Herr Ralf Dahrendorf[11] claims by contrast: 'One of the places where European decisions are increasingly being agreed (or blocked), is in the least controllable, least authorized and . . . least qualified European Institution, namely the so-called "Committee of Permanent Representatives" '.

The evidence available from the attempts to make a common energy policy is that, progressively, as the decision-making process in the Community has seized up, so expert committees have proliferated. Proposals are regularly transmitted from the Commission to the Council only to be passed back to COREPER and heard of no more. It will be remembered that the ECSC had gone some way by 1962 along the road to a common coal policy by creating a common market and common regulations; the rub came when the High Authority proposed measures to protect indigenous coal industries which would have had economic and social consequences which the governments of the member states would have had to deal with. Energy policy has not progressed substantially since that date, when the member states decided that coal policy was too important to be left to the Commission. The steady transfer of arbitration to COREPER and other institutions composed of national civil servants and away from the Council of Ministers has reduced the likelihood of measures of integration being adopted for their contribution to European political unity. In energy matters the bulk of arbitration takes place in the High-Level Working Group, and there is no political force in this environment to form a common energy policy.

E. The Political Objectives of the Commission

The Commission is not like a national civil service; it has a high degree of political sensitivity and its aim is to fashion policies, not to administer existing ones.

This is a quotation from an interview with a senior official in the Directorate-General for Energy; it offers an opinion which is probably widespread among senior officials in the Commission, especially those who have obtained seniority by working in the Commission rather than those who have been recruited recently into senior positions. But a growing minority wishes the Commission were, or thinks that it should be, less political and more like a national civil service. Anticipating later conclusions, it is likely that much of the discredit brought on the Commission from technically unsound proposals is a result of its political sensitivity. Yet we argue here that severe though the penalties are, if the Commission is to fulfil its function with any success at all it must compensate for all the odds against it by considerable political skill.

The European Treaties assign the Commission a wide range of tasks which are classified by different authors in different ways. Noël[1] identifies four functions of the Commission: it is the guardian of the Treaties, the executive arm of the Communities, the initiator of Community policy and the exponent of Community interest to the Council. There is a quality of decision-making in all these functions; it is not possible to distinguish precisely between the formation of policy and implementation; there always exists scope for judgement in the interpretation of regulations, but energy policy has not got to the stage where there are enough regulations for interpretation to matter much. The important decision-making functions are the last two: the permanent duty to initiate action by putting proposals for policy and legislation to the Council, and its presence as a non-voting participant to put the interest of the European Community before the Council of Ministers.

Coombes[2] classifies the decision-making functions of the Commission more conveniently for the present purpose as normative, initiative and mediative; the Commission decides when, what and how to initiate action, but it then has to mediate in disputes between member states and find an acceptable compromise without losing sight of the Community interest and the purpose of the initiative. In the performance of these functions the Commission and the people in it will be trying to achieve corporate and personal objectives. The public objectives of an institution, whether imposed from outside, or set from within, are not those to which the institution or people in it necessarily work in practice. It is reasonable to suppose that the principal corporate objective of the Commission will be to defend (or retrieve or extend) its power in the Community structure, in particular to defend its power of initiative against COREPER or any of the other bodies which are suggested as alternative sources. There is a variety of means by which the Commission can defend itself, but the most effective in the medium term will be to appear to promote the Community by success in getting its policies adopted; it has legal power under the Treaties to propose solutions, but to suggest good ones it requires the information necessary to understand the situation and the technical skills to assess the information, define problems and work out solutions. We have seen in preceding sections how much work the Commission has put into building up formal and informal contacts with outside experts and into extracting from member states information on trade in energy, on the pricing of primary fuels and products and on plans for investment.

There is also evidence[12] to suggest that the promotion of European integration is genuinely a leading objective of the Commission; many people working for the Commission are strongly committed to the concepts of European unity, derive personal satisfaction from its advancement and work hard to bring it about.

It follows that sectorial policies will not be designed simply to produce an optimal technical solution, but to some extent will be designed to promote the influence of the Commission and to forward the aim of European political unity.

In any particular instance the success of the Commission will be influenced by a wide variety of factors; roughly the determinants fall into two classes: those lying outside and those lying within the control of the Commission. The class outside the control of the Commission comprises the different natural endowments of the member states, the different political objectives, the natural affection of national governments for national control of events, the extent to which governments and people in the Community identify their political interest with the nation state or with the Community, the extent to which national objectives diverge and the intensity with which member states pursue their own interests. Broadly these determinants are those that determine the presence or absence of 'political will'. The other class of determinants comprises the instruments available to the Commission and the skill with which they are deployed. The technical skills of the Commission are, inevitably, no better and less specialized than those available to governments in national civil services, research centres and industries associated with the State. As we have noted, the Commission is obliged to stimulate as much collaboration with experts in member states as is possible; the prerequisite for governments of member states to take this collaboration seriously is that they should consider the matter to be politically important; from the beginning, therefore, the Commission is involved in manoeuvring for an expression of political will from member states and a political stimulus. The Commission must also try to rally support for its proposals from the specialists in member states, project for them a vision of Community ideals, transfer some of this enthusiasm to cautious national representatives and dramatize its proposals to make them appear important and appealing to a broad range of supporters. When making proposals the Commission must have a fine understanding of what is possible within each of the member states and the institutions in which they are represented; it must time its proposals effectively, judge whom they most affect and frame proposals to receive the support of affected parties without antagonizing others. The Commission must judge when to use its initiative: not to use it is as debilitating as to use it ineffectively. It must judge whether and how to combine proposals, perhaps in different fields, to balance the distribution of benefits. Sense of timing, advocacy, judgement are skills of political management without which the Commission could not get the most sublime technical proposals accepted. One might go on from there to argue that technical soundness need not be a high priority in Commission work. Although there is no logical support for this deduction, there is some evidence that the assertion accurately describes the attitudes of the Commission in some cases, especially where it is designing broad statements of policy and not specific proposals. Observations supporting this came from interviews with several officials of the Commission; one man who had come recently from industry said that he had never before seen commercial and technical considerations so subject to political considerations. Another recent recruit claimed that the Directorate-General was too much inclined to see its function as producing a 'piece of paper with political implications' and cared not what the consequences were. This hearsay evidence is given some weight by the history of the New Energy Strategy. Almost no one in the Commission would now defend the quantitative targets set in that strategy for nuclear power. It is argued that the Commission, following the oil crisis, had little opportunity to judge the technical arguments, but that they knew that the political priority was to do something to reduce the dependence on imported oil; they therefore designed a strategy which would do that, without paying much attention to whether it was technically sensible, and put it to the member states to obtain their reaction.

The basis of the policy is also defended as a first move in a session of 'Chinese bargaining', advancing an initial exaggerated proposition that can be reduced subsequently as an apparent concession. In some circumstances this may be sensible, but it is not a cool technical appraisal; the basis of the policy in this interpretation is again political, to create a strong bargaining position.

97

The policy has also been described as an exhortation to convince public opinion that it is now necessary to choose nuclear power. During the 1960s nuclear energy was less favoured on the continent than in the United Kingdom; in many countries it was almost forgotten. In Italy, for example, the last reactor went critical in 1963, and the next was planned for 1976. The Commission thought it was time to make clear the need to choose. Again, the apology for the policy is political, to exhort.

Evidently, the final choice of policy in any field will be made with a view to political objectives; commercial and technical considerations will function not as determinants, but simply as constraints. The constraints will always be more or less uncertain because of disagreement between technicians. But with nuclear energy the uncertainty in the constraints is immense; it is seen by equally responsible scientists as anything from a perfect malevolence to a perfect benevolence. In these circumstances, if political criteria do have priority within the Commission, then there is enormous scope for interpreting the technical uncertainties in the manner most suitable for the political objectives.

There are, of course, powerful political arguments against nuclear energy, but the dominant political objectives of the Commission are, I have suggested, self-preservation by demonstration of initiative in solving the problems of member states – at the time perceived as reducing imports of oil – and promotion of European unity. Generosity to nuclear energy evidently helps achieve the first objective of cutting oil imports. Promotion of European unity through nuclear energy – the 'federal power linked to the peaceful exploitation of Atomic Energy' – was the objective of Euratom, and the idea persists. Many men of talent were recruited to Euratom, imbued as well with European ideals. The institution had no significant success. Some process of natural selection operated to ensure that those who did not leave disillusioned had either found a sinecure or were compensated for lack of tangible success by joy in the exercise of technical skill in the cause of European unity. The latter class evidently comprises the people most likely to succeed within the Commission and to influence policy now. The hope that nuclear energy can promote European unity may, therefore, be just as pervasive in the Commission now as in the early days of Euratom.

Technically also, nuclear energy offers far more scope for bureaucratic control than does the oil industry, which can hinder and mitigate government control by international manoeuvring, has enormous resources, and is less favourably structured for regulation. Nuclear energy is therefore also the option most suitable for bureaucratic control; this can hardly fail to be a pleasing prospect to bureaucrats.

F. Interpretation of Technical Information According to Political Objectives

> The problem arises not from technical people, but from administrators who are sold on solutions. The administrator cannot judge technical arguments, but he knows he has to do something.

This quotation from a senior official of the Commission neatly summarizes the discussion in the last half of the preceding section. It is certainly the explanation offered within the Commission for the lack of technical conviction in the proposals for nuclear power in the New Strategy. Rumour in the Commission has it that the figures in that document were produced in an afternoon from the following logic. It is politically unacceptable to restrain energy use; estimate, therefore, the unrestricted growth of energy demand; estimate the possibility of reducing demand by more efficient use; estimate the possible increase in production of indigenous oil; do the same for gas and coal; judge what is the maximum dependence on imported fuels that is tolerable. The remaining demand is then to be met by the marginal source of supply, which is nuclear. This defines the size of the nuclear programme.

So strong is the belief in the Commission that the policy was designed rapidly, by a small group of people with political rather than technical priorities, that it seems impossible not to accept the broad truth of the hearsay. But even if that were so, it does not follow that the technical people are absolved from blame. The formulation of a complex policy cannot be accurately described by a linear series of decisions such as that sketched above for the case of the New Strategy; the earlier steps depend for consistency on some knowledge of what the later steps will be. In this particular case the judgement of what dependence on imported fuels is tolerable is influenced by a prior notion of the biggest conceivable effort that the Community could make in constructing nuclear plant and the commercial competitiveness of the output from that plant. Euratom was founded on excessively optimistic forecasts of the future for nuclear energy, and this attitude persisted in Community thought so that in 1972, before the oil crisis, the Commission was still tentatively proposing 'a nuclear generating capacity of 200 GW(e), by the middle of the next decade'.[13]

In fact, the 200 GW(e) of the New Strategy, supposedly a political response to the oil crisis, was already advocated by the Commission before the crisis, although not emphasized. Rather than the technologists of the Commission reluctantly producing technical arguments to shore up the obsessions of the policy makers, the process operating seems to be more akin to collusion.

The enthusiasts for nuclear energy, a technology which, as we have seen, accords well with the political objectives of the Commission, create high expectations within the Commission. Personally the enthusiast will, as is only human, entertain great ambitions for his preferred technology. Normally he would be restrained to some extent in his advocacy by commercial, economic and political criteria. If, however, the political environment in which he works reinforces his personal assessment and simultaneously suspends commercial and economic criteria, then the opportunities for extreme beliefs are favourable. This process by which political objectives and beliefs operate to modify perceptions of technical constraints is universal in individuals and institutions. Within many institutions personal idiosyncracies to some extent cancel out, and within the vast majority of institutions the urgent responsibility for real resources or the responsibility to an electorate, to an elected body or to shareholders act to restrain idiosyncratic interpretations of situations by threatening financial loss or loss of power. The characteristics of the Commission are such that there are only weak constraints on collusion. The characteristics of nuclear energy can be presented in such a way as to match the political objectives of the Commission so well that, instead of personal idiosyncracies cancelling each other out, they can reinforce each other and a common collusion can develop. There is certainly remarkably little sign of a power struggle between fuels in the Directorate-General for Energy; some of the most vigorous argument in favour of nuclear energy is to be found in the oil and coal directorates. Nor is the Commission unduly restrained by any responsibility for real resources or responsibility to an elected body. If an electricity supply industry builds far too much nuclear generating capacity then it has to bear the financial consequences itself; no such spectre haunts the Commission. The only constraint on the advocacy of poor technical solutions for political reasons is the long-term requirement to maintain the credibility of the Directorate-General for Energy. This is not, perhaps, a strong constraint.

Technical expertise in the energy sector is conveniently classified by fuel sources: coal, hydrocarbons, nuclear energy. Synthesis of this information is then made on economic and political criteria; the organization of the Directorate-General for Energy does indeed contain elements with an economic and political function. One may well criticize the political priorities of the Commission in energy policy for neglecting the risks of proliferation of fissile material, for neglecting the significance of storing fission products, for retreating from conflict with coal lobbies in member states, and on other grounds; there is, however, no doubt that the function of political synthesis is active. The function of economic synthesis seems, in contrast, to be extraordinarily inactive. One of the most striking aspects of the New Strategy was its commercial implausibility; this is discussed in detail later but, briefly, the estimates of growth in electricity demand were simple and unlikely extrapolations, the cost of nuclear power in the tasks envisaged for it were not discussed at all, and the difficulties of penetrating these markets were ignored. An extreme example of this was the short-lived proposal for 20 MW(e) equivalent of process heat from nuclear energy by 1985. There was not the remotest shadow of argument to show where or how this would be commercially viable. It appears that the Commission is now trying to improve its analysis of the future energy market by constructing a European energy model. It is debatable just how useful these large models are; simple transparent calculations incorporating the main features are perhaps less likely to be grossly misleading. But in any case, it is fair to say that greater attention to commercial constraints might help offset the deleterious consequences of the Commission's quite justifiable political sensitivity.

The Commission does not measure its success by technical or commercial criteria, but instead by the extent to which it persuades member states to do the things it thinks should be done. But even to satisfy this criterion in the long run, the proposals must be technically and commercially competent.

References
1. Emile Noël, *Working Together* (Commission of the European Communities, January 1975).
2. D. Coombes, *Politics and Bureaucracy in the European Community* (Allen and Unwin, 1970).
3. P. Gerbet and D. Pepy (Ed.), *La décision dans les Communautés Européennes* (Institut d'Etudes Européennes, Université Libre de Bruxelles, 1969).
4. *Authorisation Procedure for the Construction and Operation of Nuclear Installations within the EEC Member States.* Report prepared by J. M. Ridier and Associates, Commission of the European Communities, Brussels, 1974); see also:
   Working Document on a Community Policy on the Siting of Nuclear Power Stations (Committee on Energy, Research and Technology, European Parliament, September 1975).
5. *Proposal for a Council decision adopting a research and training programme for the safety of nuclear installations, Com(75)523* (Brussels, October 1975).
6. *Proposal for a Council decision adopting a research and training programme for the EAEC on fast breeder reactors, Com(75)524* (Brussels, October 1975).
7. *Première orientation pour une politique énergétique communautaire* (Commission of the European Communities, Brussels, 1968).
8. *Towards a new energy policy strategy for the European Community* (*Bulletin of the European Communities, Supplement 4/74*, Brussels, 1974).
9. *Situation and Prospects of the Industries Producing Heavy Electrical Engineering and Nuclear Equipment for Electricity Generating in the Community* (Working Paper of the Commission, July 1975).

10. Emile Noël, 'The Committee of Permanent Representatives', *Journal of Common Market Studies 5*, (1967).
11. R. Dahrendorf, 'Wieland Europa', *Die Zeit*, 9 July 1971, translated and reprinted in *European Integration*, Ed. Michael Hodges (Penguin, 1972).
12. R. L. Peterson, *Career Motivation of Administrators and their Impact in the European Community* (The Social Science Foundation and Graduate School of International Studies Monograph Series in World Affairs, University of Denver).
13. *Guidelines and Priority Actions Under the Community Energy Policy* (*Bulletin of the European Communities*, 1973).

III

Present Perception of Policy

A. General Concepts

The Community energy policy contained in *Towards a New Energy Strategy*[1] and later papers[2-8] is in no way a final opinion; it is a stage in the evolution of a Community energy policy and may be changed to accommodate special concerns of member states or to cope with new events in the world. However, the general concepts on which it was built have been established for a long time as central to Community policy; the nature and history of these concepts have been described already; briefly they are:

(a) it is politically quite unacceptable to restrain economic growth or to manage the form which growth takes by restricting energy-use artificially; actions of this nature would hinder the efforts of the economic community to make its people ever wealthier;

(b) to preserve economic and political security it is necessary to restrict imports of fuel, especially oil, and to arrange that the remaining imports come from as many different countries as possible;

(c) alternatives to imported fuel must be found, namely:
   (i) greater output from indigenous sources of coal, oil and gas;
   (ii) a more efficient use of energy;
   (iii) subsidized alternatives such as coal and nuclear energy.

(d) it is important to recognize, and benefit from, the interdependence of consumers and producers, especially the natural relationship of the EEC and the Middle East;

(e) implicit in the policy are certain political preoccupations of the Commission and ideas about the nature of European integration. The idea behind the Community is to progress eventually to a federal or confederal power in Europe. Energy policy is not as important in itself as for the distortions which it now causes in industrial competition within the Community and, even more importantly, for its significance in the bigger problem of who will take the decisions about the future of Europe. If decisions are taken by outsiders, this is a serious loss, because however convincing may be the façade of détente and dialogue, eventually the realities of power win through. It is essential to restore a reasonable measure of power to European decision-making centres. Therefore a common policy on energy is predicated more for political gain than commercial gain, and member states should adopt common measures even though the commercial gains are not evident.

The political orientation of the Directorate-General for Energy appears to have been much as above during the time when M. Ferdinand Spaak was Director-General; the son of M. Paul-Henri Spaak and a dedicated European, he apparently held strongly to the opinion that energy policy should be an integrative force in the Community and not simply a means of co-ordinating national policies. The departure of M. Spaak as Community representative to Washington, and the appointment of a Director-General from the U.K., may introduce different ideas about the nature of European energy policy, and possibly shift the political emphasis of the Directorate-General. The different ideas that may now be pressed more powerfully are those that are customarily styled 'pragmatic'. 'Pragmatists' might argue that energy is being tackled adequately for the most part on a national basis; there is no great gain, for example, from unifying or managing the oil companies. The Commission should instead try to shift energy policy at the margin; for example, it would be sensible to promote the burning of indigenous coal in the Community because if left to member states the consumption of coal would fall away; a Community policy to determine how much coal should be protected and at whose expense is therefore necessary. Another specific area in which the Commission could well seek to have a marginal effect is in providing Community finance for projects which member states are willing to permit, but for which they have no money – for example nuclear power stations in Italy or North Sea oil if it were necessary. A pragmatist would also advise spending less time defending those achievements of the past which have little technical significance, but great symbolic value to European idealists. For example, the Euratom Treaty was drawn up to deal with a situation which never materialized and the institution it established was never appropriate. To some people to whom integration is a high priority the Euratom Treaty enshrines solid achievements which are too rare things to abandon. Obsession with details of an inappropriate Treaty setting up a largely defunct institution inhibits the creation of an appropriate policy for the present.

The nature of European integration and its relevance to energy policy may therefore be the source of more evenly matched debate within the Commission in the future than it has been in the past. There are external determinants supporting both sides. The inertia of member states can always be relied on by the pragmatists. The chief hope of the Europeans must be that international initiatives in the IEA will force the Community to define an energy policy in order that it can participate as a Community. The resistance of France to all aspects of the IEA does not encourage this hope.

In the following sections I shall try to describe what might be the contributions of various fuels to achieving the objectives described. The description purports to be roughly the opinions prevailing in the Commission. Obviously the Commission contains a wide range of opinion; no generalization of this sort is completely satisfactory even in principle, and in practice distortion no doubt also creeps in.

B. Nuclear Energy

1. THE EXPLANATION OF EARLIER FAILURES

In the late 1950s and the early 1960s, the future of nuclear energy appeared assured. Leadtimes for plant were about five years, short by present standards, and the problems of financing and forecasting demand were not severe. There was no supply problem for uranium. Public opinion had not reacted to the consequences of waste disposal and the proliferation of fissile material. The question was 'Is nuclear energy competitive?' The basis for forecasting the cost of nuclear energy was weak; the technology was uncertain, safety standards were uncertain, variation of cost between reactor types and according to size was uncertain. The United Kingdom, France and Germany built commercial prototype reactors. The conclusion was that only very large-scale plant would be competitive because the capital cost was a crucial element of the financial appraisal, and it was essential to obtain as much economy of scale as was technically feasible. Fuel oil at the time was dependable and available at a low price; there was little incentive to go on with difficult and capital-intensive nuclear projects. At the end of 1973 the price of fuel oil exploded and suddenly the economic superiority of nuclear energy became apparent. It was now possible to justify nuclear energy for almost all electricity generation.

2. THE BASIS FOR TARGETS

The addition of national forecasts of installed nuclear generating capacity for 1985 gave 160 MW(e). The Nuclear Directorate of the Directorate-General for Energy, in a position to see the whole European scene, proposed 200 MW(e) of generating capacity, based on projections of electricity supply, and 20 MW(e) for process heat. There appears to have been strong protest from parts of the Directorate-General for Industry that the manufacturing industry could never cope. But the driving force for the proposal was the political decision to provide as much energy as possible from nuclear fuels. The proposals were therefore re-examined to see how the rate of installation of nuclear plant could be hastened by standardization of reactor design, safety measures and radiological protection. The conclusion of this study was that the Community was capable of this enormous effort in nuclear energy if French and German reactor designs were standardized and made as similar as possible.[9] The conceptually legitimate origin of the 40 MW(e) addition to the sum of national programmes by 1985 is the benefit of specialization within an economic community. The joint basis for the proposals was, therefore, that growth in electricity supply would permit this nuclear capacity; it was now economic and the Community was capable of the effort.

There are a number of objections to this proposal. The finance of the programme, the supply of uranium, the storage of fission products and the proliferation of fissile materials are dealt with in later sections; these are difficult matters to assess and have a considerable political content. But there are also more straightforward industrial and commercial objections. The programme makes substantial demands on the design and engineering resources of the Community which, despite the Commission's assurance, some think greater than available capacity; the engineers may not be available for the programme; operators for power stations may not be available and the market for electricity may not be there.

Strictly in terms of industrial capacity the Commission does make a good case that Europe has resources enough to match a very big effort in nuclear power – provided the industries have sufficient warning and confidence to invest in time. A few weaknesses in the industrial chain have been identified, either because production capacity for certain critical components in the Community would be inadequate to meet rising demand or because although production facilities appear adequate they lie outside the Community. In the first place careful planning and selective investment should ensure continuity of supply. It is said that *Electricité de France* is confident that its own programme is industrially sound, and French opinion on energy matters, especially nuclear energy, carries considerable weight in the Commission.

Just now some components cannot be produced in the Community; for example, steel blocks of the size required to make alternator motors above 900 MVA must be imported from the U.S.A. or Japan. There are no presses in the Community that will make the very thick, large-diameter seamless forged rings and flanges for the pressure vessels in LWRs; at present these come from Japan. It is is not clear that the manufacture of these components is likely to restrict the nuclear programme but the Commission feels strongly that they should be manufactured in the Community.[9]

The Commission has also investigated the requirements for trained engineers and operators; it is argued that the number of trained engineers required does not increase proportionately to the size of the programme (mainly because of the high degree of standardization), and that a shortage of skilled workmen, such as skilled welders for high pressure vessels, is more likely. The training of people to operate power stations is not seen as a serious obstacle; it takes less time to train the people than to build the power station, and the level of training is no higher than for many other modern jobs, such as airline pilots.

It does seem that with suitable investment (requiring confidence and warning) it may well be possible to build and operate the number of reactors proposed. There are some other points to bear in mind in this context. Europe is up to now an exporter of electrical generating plant, and this manufacturing capacity can be switched to an internal market. Continental Europe, particularly Germany, has a strong industrial structure. Germany was able to free itself from American licences two or three years ago and to develop a German concept of a reactor, which it then sold abroad against American competition. Finally, the programme relies heavily on rigorous standardization. France has already got rid of the BWR after the recent reorganization of its nuclear industry. Germany also shows a clear preference for the PWR. The chance of an integrated European nuclear industry, lost when the U.K. chose the SGHWR, may come again if the U.K. abandons the SGHWR in favour of American designs, as is now mooted even by the UKAEA.

Although the programme may be technically possible, it may not be easy to mobilize the financial resources, partly because of the sheer size of the investment, but mainly because it is not clear that the investment is secure.

The financial support that would be necessary for the nuclear programme, possible sources and possible Community action, have been preoccupations of the Commission for some time. The large increase in duty on Middle Eastern oil might in itself be expected to attract more money to nuclear energy because it is obviously a more profitable proposition than before. Curiously, this is not necessarily so. If, before the sudden rise in Middle Eastern oil prices, the marginal returns on capital were broadly similar for investment in nuclear energy and investment in alternative sources of oil, then after the rise in energy prices the rate of return on capital for the capital-intensive option (nuclear) will rise less quickly than the rate of return for the option requiring less initial outlay (alternative sources of oil). A rise in energy prices may then tend to divert funds away from capital-intensive projects. The consequences could be disastrous. Even though temporarily the direct dependence on the Middle East is alleviated, the economic dominance of oil in general is strengthened; indirectly, therefore, the economic and political strength of the major producers will be enhanced. When the new sources of oil are exhausted the investment in nuclear energy will not have been made, and dependence on the Middle East will be complete. It is difficult to know to what extent this analysis is valid, but there is certainly some truth in it. The oil crisis has provoked much new investment in the oil industry, and although many plans for nuclear power have been announced, by no means all of them have been implemented. It may well be that the flow of money into nuclear energy has not really accelerated since the oil crisis.

Consequently, if nuclear power is to be developed as rapidly as is technically possible and politically advisable, it is important, in the view of the Commission, that the technology be encouraged by bodies such as itself examining events against a distant time horizon. The Commission's proposals for Community finance for nuclear power are, therefore, central to its policy.[10]

Apart from the greater financial attraction of other energy options, it can also be argued that much proposed investment in nuclear energy is simply not profitable even after the rise in oil prices because:

(a) it may well be that the electricity cannot be easily marketed;
(b) supplies of uranium over the lifetime of the reactor cannot be guaranteed;
(c) public opposition may slow down the licensing and construction of reactors and impede their operation.

3. URANIUM SUPPLY

A rough idea of what the implications of the nuclear programme might be for the supply and reprocessing of fissile fuels is given by the 'reference model' in *Towards a Community Nuclear Fuel Supply Policy*,[6] one of the supporting documents to *Objectives for 1985*.[2]

Nuclear Operating Capacity
(GW(e))

	1975	1980	1985	1990
Proven reactors	25	64	194	360
Fast reactors	—	1	5	20
HTRs	—	—	1	20
TOTAL	25	65	200	400

Uranium Requirement
('000 metric tons)

	1975	1980	1985
Uranium oxide	5.5	23	50
SWU	1.7	10	25
Reprocessing	0.1	1	3

The paper then calculates the annual and cumulative requirements of proposed nuclear programmes throughout the world up to 1990.

Uranium Oxide Requirements
('000 metric tons)

	1973	1975	1980	1985	1990
Annual requirement	17	26	66	127	224
Cumulative requirement	17	64	297	799	1713

It compares this with present production in the world, which is 15,000 tonnes per year, and with various measures of total reserves; for example, reasonably assured resources up to $10 per lb U_3O_8 are estimated at 947,000 tonnes, a much more uncertain estimate of resources that may be recoverable up to $15 per lb is 3.25 million tonnes. The twin problems are clearly to expand production very rapidly (by 10 times in 15 years) and to discover new deposits equally rapidly.

The physical availability of nuclear fuels does not seem to be considered a serious problem in the Commission. It is argued that supplies have been procured to cover requirements up to 1985. Historically uranium prices have been depressed by glut following over-estimates of demand in the 1950s and early 1960s; the incentive to explore was therefore low. The present price level provides an incentive to explore, to develop technology for using poorer ores and to improve the exploitation of ores now being worked. The result of this is that there may be an uncomfortable period after 1985 and in the early 1990s, but after that the renewed incentives will begin to produce results.

This is a classical economic argument, and none the worse for that. Against it one can argue that a nuclear reactor will have a life expectancy of 30 years, and that one should therefore look not at the cumulative requirements for uranium up to 1990, but at the requirements over their lifetime of the capacity built in 1990; this comes to something like six million tonnes of U_3O_8, twice the uncertain estimate of resources recoverable up to $15 per lb. There is a well-known morass of argument and counter-argument at the confluence of these two lines of reasoning; only time will show what is correct. What we can say is that because of the financial risk of investment in nuclear plant, decisions will only be made to proceed if fuel is reasonably assured over much of the future for each individual project. It may well be that the availability of fuel will restrict the size of nuclear programmes, but it will not come as a surprise and will not lead to generating capacity having to be scrapped for lack of fuel. Supplies of fuel may eventually restrict programmes, and one cannot count, therefore, on arbitrary projections of nuclear capacity, but shortage of fuel is not an argument for not going on with such reactors as can be reasonably assured of supplies.

The other important processes in the fuel cycle appear to have received less attention, partly because the published documents deal only with policy and its consequential requirements up to 1985. By that time the bulk of the nuclear capacity proposed would only recently have been commissioned and the cumulative demand on such services as uranium enrichment and fuel reprocessing would be small. The Commission is relying to some extent on enrichment from outside the Community – the principal suppliers are keen to enrich their own fuel in any case. The lead time for enrichment plant, which is considered as comparatively simple and proven technology, is probably sufficiently short for shortages to be avoided at a later stage. The availability of reprocessing plant is a different matter. There is no proven commercial technique for reprocessing uranium oxide fuel. There is no commercial reprocessing capacity for oxide fuel in continental Europe. The French have taken the lead and may be able to reprocess 800 tons a year by the end of the 1970s – but it may not work.

4. POLITICAL CONSEQUENCES

We have discussed how well nuclear energy suits the political objectives of the Commission. Here we examine how the Commission views some of the less attractive political consequences, which we take to comprise mainly public opposition to the operation of reactors, the disposal of waste products and the proliferation of fissile materials.

Public Opposition: There can be no doubt that the operation of nuclear reactors and the processing and disposal of fission products raise problems which are viewed much more seriously by some national governments than by the Commission. The objectionable effects of a nuclear programme of the magnitude proposed were quite inadequately discussed in the 1974 papers. They were hardly treated much better in the lengthy *Second Illustrative Nuclear Programme for the Community*, published in 1972.[11] The problems are subsumed under the heading 'Conditions required for the achievement of the programme', indicating quite clearly that they are not regarded as a constraint to nuclear programmes, but as second order effects to be cleared up.

The Directorate-General for Energy observes: 'As regards the anxiety about the storage of radioactive waste, it can be stressed that this problem is not yet acute and that adequate solutions will have been found by the time they are needed.[1]

In fairness to the Directorate-General for Energy, the consequences of managing or disposing of radioactive waste are very difficult to think about intelligently. All we can do with any certainty is describe the attitude of the various interested parties. The Commission is quite sanguine about the matter, as is the French Government. The United Kingdom Government has reservations, but the United Kingdom pro-gramme is so small that public opposition is not strong and unlikely to be a serious constraint. West German electricity supply companies have a large combined programme of nuclear power, but the government has recently indicated that it will only authorize further stations in the programme if a satisfactory way is found of dealing with the nuclear waste. Germany has no reprocessing capacity of her own at present and probably will not have any operating before the late 1980s. The only measures available until then are storing the irradiated fuel elements or sending them to France or the United Kingdom for reprocessing. The former alternative does not seem to be encouraged by the government; application by the operators to increase the storage capacity at the Biblis site was recently refused. The second alternative arouses opposition in the countries to whom the fuel is to be sent. There is some resistance in the United Kingdom, and to a much lesser degree in France, to the expansion of reprocessing capacity for any purpose, but especially for reprocessing fuel elements for foreign nuclear stations. The extent to which West Germany can implement its plans for nuclear power may depend on opinion in the United Kingdom and France.

Intentions in the smaller countries of the Communities are conditional in some way on satisfactory solutions to the environmental problems, especially the disposal of waste. The Belgian Government have given approval to a ten-year programme, but they have reserved final judgement and will review the situation at the end of that period. The Netherlands have a tiny programme, and even that they have until 1977 to decide upon. Denmark has no definite programme at all. The Netherlands, Italy and Denmark all have substantial internal opposition. The governments of these countries are often ambivalent in their attitude; although they to some extent reflect the opposition of their electorate in the Community forum, they also attempt to push nuclear programmes at home under the shelter of the Community. One of the ancillary reasons for the ambitious targets of the New Energy Strategy was to help member states such as the Netherlands and Italy, who have difficulty getting nuclear programmes through their parliaments because of strong anti-nuclear lobbies. The idea was to provide some solidarity among governments of nuclear states so that the affected countries could in part lay the blame on the Community. In contrast to the

111

ambivalence at this end of the spectrum, at the pro-nuclear end France is entirely dedicated to her own nuclear programme and to obtaining assistance for nuclear projects from the Community.

Proliferation: As more countries acquire the technology of commercial nuclear power, so they will inevitably acquire access to the technology of thermonuclear weapons. Enrichment plant can be run to produce weapon grade uranium, reprocessing plant extracts plutonium from spent fuel elements as a matter of course; some small reactors contain fuel elements fabricated from highly enriched uranium that could make a thermonuclear weapon of no great explosive power but with thoroughly unpleasant radioactive products.

The Commission's proposals for energy policy exacerbate this situation in two different but reinforcing ways. Firstly, a large commercial programme in Europe will seek to alleviate fluctuations in domestic demand or make up for shortfalls by selling abroad. Any mechanism for safeguarding the transfer of strategic materials or technology will come under extreme pressure. There is little evidence from the history of arms sales by the U.K. and, especially, France to suggest that member states would resist short-term commercial gain in order to avoid creating enormous political problems unless they could be assured that no other country would reap the same gain and present them in any case with the same problems. Solidarity among nuclear exporting countries should therefore be a first priority, and the Commission has an obligation to initiate the drafting of a code of conduct for member states of the European Community. Secondly, the special relationship between the oil producers of the Middle East and the European Community is likely to make the European Community an equally special source of proliferation. One assurance to the Middle East that they do not prejudice their own future in running down their oil reserves is for the European states to sell them nuclear technology; the symbiosis is almost perfect. There is a basis for arguing that nuclear power is even now an economic option in the Middle East despite their enormous supplies of oil. The argument runs as follows: fuel oil has to be got rid of, and is therefore sold in Europe at a price which just breaks even with nuclear power for electricity production; if the Middle East countries limit production to conserve their resources, then the value of fuel oil to them is what they can sell it for in Europe minus the cost of freight; nuclear energy is therefore more or less as competitive for electricity production in the Middle East as in Europe. In addition to this not wholly convincing economic argument, there are the obvious matters of long-term, prestige and military benefits, and technological experience which will ensure a demand in the Middle East for nuclear imports. Europe, being the largest customer for oil, flaunting its own ambitious nuclear programme and claiming a special relationship with the Middle East, is the obvious and eager supplier. It seems universally accepted in the Commission that this is part of the price that Europe will eventually have to pay for oil. Again, one would imagine the Commission had an obligation to examine the conditions on which this transfer should take place.

In fact, the Commission's record on the matter is appalling. There is dissension about how hard it has actually tried, but certainly nothing has been made public. The New Strategy[1] and the Second Illustrative Programme[11] are quite silent on the subject. An apology for the Commission claims that essentially such problems are not well covered by the written framework of the Community – the Treaty of Rome is obscure and there has not been enough power in the Commission to take any initiative. The Commission was discouraged by the history of its efforts to co-ordinate the nuclear industry and harmonize safety standards, in which matters it was perpetually frustrated by member states. Tentative attempts were made by the Commission to discover the attitudes of member states to safeguards, but they got nowhere before the London agreement. The Commission lost the initiative again and member states once more demonstrated a preference for seeking solutions outside the Community.

5. OUTCOME OF PROPOSALS

By May 1976 the sum of national nuclear programmes to 1985 had declined to 125 GW(e), and the Commission's appraisal of the underlying trend was that less than 100 MW(e) would actually be built.

The failure to achieve the 160 GW(e) which was the sum of national programmes and which was the target agreed by the Council of Ministers, let alone the Commission's target of 200 GW(e), is attributed to an unforeseen slow down in electricity growth and to mounting public opposition. Just as experts always thought oil would be available at historic prices, so it was thought, argues the Commission, that the rate of increase in electricity demand would not fall. To have the 8 or 9 per cent growth in electricity consumption which is implicit in the nuclear proposals, electricity must be sold for heat. The state-owned electricity supply authority in France launched a campaign of 'toute électrique' and the state co-operated by installing electric heating in new state housing. The campaign has not been altogether successful partly because electricity is not a competitive source of heat. Moreover, the oil companies have attempted to squeeze out nuclear energy, much as they succeeded in doing with coal, by selling the heavy fuel oil left from refining at prices calculated just to undercut alternative sources of fuel for electricity generation. Therefore, despite the rise in crude oil prices, nuclear energy has not had the unchallenged entry into power genera-

113

tion foreseen for it at the end of 1973. Roughly, this is the apology for failure to achieve the nuclear objectives.

C. Hydrocarbons

1. RELATIONSHIP WITH OIL PRODUCERS

It is argued that the producers of oil need a long-term income to establish their countries as diversified industrial powers; and that the consumers need secure supplies of oil until fast reactors and fission bring them to the point at which capital investment provides unlimited power. This mutual need is obscured by insecurity on both sides: the producers feel that they are regarded as pirates by the consumers, and that therefore obligations undertaken by consuming countries and companies may not be honoured; and the consumers fear that interruptions in supply may be inflicted on them as a political reprisal. Having recognized their complementary needs, the two sides should develop a stable relationship by a variety of means. The Euro-Arab dialogue was designed by the Europeans for this purpose.

In a similar way, it is important that the mutual requirements of the consumers and producers be clear to one another. If the consuming countries succeed in persuading the producing countries that they will develop indigenous resources and more efficient techniques for using energy and will therefore need only a certain quantity of oil, and if the consumers do not succeed with their proposals, then oil will not be available to make up the deficiency, because the producers will not have made the necessary investment in transportation, pipelines, port facilities and, to a lesser extent, in exploration and production. Historically, the oil companies invested ahead of time, probably to ensure surplus capacity in the producing countries and to inhibit producer cartels, but with the effect of maintaining continuous downward pressure on prices. If in the future the investment is not made until demand is real then the pressures on prices will be upward.

In both these undertakings, the recognition and clarification of a mutual dependence, the EEC is an appropriate unit; negotiation as a Community avoids competition between member states.

A common commercial agreement – for example, a Community agency with monopoly purchasing rights – is a quite different topic on which opinion is divided. It is argued that Europe, being the largest importer of oil in the world, would have great influence on the market if she were to form one or two purchasing organizations with exclusive rights to purchase hydrocarbons from outside the Community. By this means the Community could easily supervise the structure of oil imports and ensure that it was not dangerously biased to particular sources; the arrangement would also facilitate Community control of the distri-

114

bution of available imports in times when supplies were scarce; the weight of the organization as buyers in the market would permit them to negotiate lower prices than those obtained by a multitude of buyers through the intermediary oil companies who have no great interest in low prices. Whatever the merit of the case, it is not supported by any national government: to the U.K. and Germany the idea is too interventionist; France is reluctant to antagonize the oil producers by forming consumer organizations – although, interestingly enough, the economic support for the idea is similar to the arguments which France used in 1953 to show why her coal purchasing monopoly, ATIC, should not be reorganized before first breaking up the German coal-selling monopoly, GEORG.

2. NATURAL GAS

The production of natural gas from the enormous Groningen field has helped the EEC to become 94 per cent self-sufficient in this fuel; the small deficit is made up from Algeria and the U.S.S.R. Of the gas from Groningen 62.6 per cent is presently exported from the Netherlands to other Community countries, but production from Groningen is expected to peak in 1978, and the Dutch already have plans to start reducing exports in 1978 and to stop them completely by 1994 when the last of the present long-term contracts expire. Natural gas from Groningen has been available at prices well below c.i.f. parity with oil, and this has had two principal consequences. Firstly, it led to an exceedingly wasteful use of a premium fuel. In 1974, 12.2 per cent of the production from Groningen was burnt in power stations and another 12.7 per cent went to large factories mainly to be used as bulk fuel. Gasunie (the 10 per cent state-owned natural gas utility in the Netherlands) now plans to restrict future sales as far as possible to premium uses and gradually to reduce rates to power stations and for bulk heat. The second consequence of the low price was that it permitted a rapid expansion of natural gas usage in Western Europe. The necessary infrastructure for transmission and distribution was financed out of the still generous profit to the supplier and the benefit of the low price permitted the user to reinvest in natural gas using equipment. In some ways this was wasteful, but it did mean that an entirely new energy supply option was created for Europe. Even if imports of natural gas will not now be available much below c.i.f. parity with oil, they are still an attractive proposition because the necessary infrastructure exists. World reserves of natural gas are large; the Institute for Gas Technology in the U.S.A. estimates that total renewable reserves could sustain a 4 per cent increase in production for the next 50 years. Because of this the Commission is keen to encourage the further use of natural gas and in its objectives for 1985[2] proposed that consumption of natural gas should be tripled over the next 10 years. Consumption in 1973 was 117 million tons oil equivalent (mtoe); it was proposed to step up Community production on land and offshore to 225 mtoe if possible and to secure up to 115 mtoe from non-member countries. The figure for imports was obtained by summing all known, probable and possible contracts in member states, even where these were mutually exclusive preliminary negotiations for the same source. The figure for indigenous production is also optimistic. Nevertheless, the Commission is quite correct in drawing attention to the advantages of natural gas.

An aspect of increased use of natural gas in Europe which is not given overt attention in the Commission's publications, but which cannot be other than prominent in their thinking, is the potential of the U.S.S.R. The U.S.S.R. probably possesses the largest reserve of natural gas in the world. Some of these reserves are in relatively accessible and settled regions such as the Ukraine and around the Caspian Sea. These sources are for the most part past their peak and Soviet effort is now shifting to the very rich, but very inhospitable and remote region in Western Siberia near and beyond the Arctic Circle. This region contains five out of the 11 gas fields in the world which are thought to contain more than 10^{12} cubic metres of gas.

The cost of developing these resources has been, and will continue to be, enormous; the chief beneficiaries will be the Soviet consumer and industry and the Comecon countries who are participating directly in the construction of pipelines to transport natural gas to the industrial centres of Eastern Europe. But the Soviet Union lacks hard foreign currency and almost certainly also intends to export large quantities of this gas production. The export programme is already developed. Contracts for the delivery of more than 20×10^9 cubic metres of natural gas per year to Western Europe by 1980 have already been agreed, with 10×10^9 cubic metres going to West Germany and 4×10^9 cubic metres going to France. Some of these contracts are long term and will not expire until after A.D. 2000.

Evidently the enormous reserves of natural gas in the U.S.S.R. are an attractive source of energy to the member states of the Community. Equally evidently there are substantial uncertainties. The amount of gas available depends partly on the difference between Soviet production and demand from the Comecon countries; both are difficult to estimate and the difference between them is most uncertain. It also depends partly on what intentions the Soviet Union has to become a principal exporter of energy, which again are obscure. Finally there is the political risk of dependence on a Communist state for a commodity of the greatest strategic importance; the clarity with which the risk can be perceived does not help assess the degree of dependence to be tolerated.

The European natural gas network could also be used to carry substitute natural gas (SNG). This can be manufactured from coal at a cost in excess of present c.i.f. prices of natural gas and in excess of present c.i.f. parity prices for oil. Nevertheless, there is a case for making SNG and the argument is given a run later on.

3. INTERVENTION IN THE MARKET

The guiding principle of the Common Market was to eliminate all artificial impediments to the healthy cut and thrust of commercial competition. Energy, in particular oil products, has always hindered the pursuit of this principle. Most obviously, different taxes and duties on hydrocarbons in member states distort competition. In principle this can be rectified simply by harmonizing taxes, but since in practice national taxes on energy are the result of attempts to raise revenue and steer energy and industrial policy, efforts to change them are bound to meet with opposition.

Less obviously, the vertically integrated structure of the oil industries and the dominance of the market by a few companies could easily lead to agreements between companies and concerted practices to manipulate prices and squeeze out smaller undertakings. The reports of the Commission on Competition Policy before and after the oil crisis are much concerned with this matter.[12,13]

Then again, the application by member states, after the oil crisis, of national regulations to the price of oil products immediately made some national markets more attractive than others to the oil companies – leading eventually to distortions of competition.

Generally in Europe the extent of government control of the oil companies is increasing. Up to 1970/71 it was not thought necessary in some Community countries to have control over oil policy other than that given by taxation; Belgium, Germany, Denmark and the United Kingdom essentially considered free markets to be adequate. Some countries, such as France and Italy, exercise extensive control over the oil companies. The Commission, largely because of French influence in its planning philosophy, has always considered it necessary to control the oil companies and regulate the oil industry. Lately its case has been strengthened, as national governments have increasingly interfered in their oil markets. The United Kingdom has greatly extended its control over the oil industry by creating a State Oil Company and is taking statutory powers to direct investment in the North Sea, to control output, and to participate in operations. Germany has begun to build a national oil policy around a state oil company. If governments really perceive their future as European then, the Commission argues, they should co-ordinate their intervention. Since in the Common Market products must circulate freely, it is absurd for a country to control prices; if prices are to be controlled it should be at a Community level. In fact the Council has agreed to monitor prices. The prices of oil products will be reported to the Commission and analysed; if it appears that there are distortions, for example that prices may rise due to a deficit in supplies, then the Commission will propose the measures needed to control prices and member countries will adopt them together. The Council has to give its consent to the measures and will not necessarily do so, but it is a beginning.

4. TECHNICAL CO-ORDINATION

There are a number of attractive possibilities for co-ordinating the hydrocarbon policies of member states, particularly for increasing communal security and for joint research programmes.

Communal security of supply is improved by interlocking energy supply systems. For example, one restriction on the expansion of natural gas markets within the community using imported gas is the danger of a cut in supply. If West Germany wishes to buy gas from the U.S.S.R. it may be inhibited because the supply is not politically secure. If the West German natural gas system were linked effectively to other community countries then the risk might be shared; the shared risk might be acceptable and a new supply option would be created. Clearly it might be possible to arrange this as a commercial proposition between two countries, but the more the members of the group the more flexible the system, and some central planning seems desirable. Moreover, to react successfully in a crisis requires some form of political unity such as might be expected of the Community. There are, of course, technical limitations on the extent to which systems carrying gas of different calorific value can be integrated.

Similarly, as more gas is imported, more gas is required to provide security. Gas is difficult to store. Most good sites for geological storage are in France, where the potential aquifer storage is large and simple. In an integrated natural gas system France could provide storage for the Community.

The same principle applies to the gas basins in the North Sea; they have good porosity and good permeability; they could provide storage capacity. But in that case why deplete them now, why not import gas through a Channel link and view the gas basins as strategic storage capacity for the Community? Maintenance costs are not excessive in the southern part of the North Sea. It is not a conceivable practice for oil reservoirs further north because the investment is higher, the weather poor, the platforms unsuitable and maintenance costs astronomic.

Similarly for oil, common technical standards for products would facilitate the exchange of products in times of crisis to equalize misery.

The Community can also act together to support research – an established function of international bodies. It has already created a fund to assist industry by loans for developing new technology; it proposes specifically projects for deep sea exploration in participation with oil companies. The rationale for this is that the European states have a greater interest in offshore exploration than the oil companies, and by this means they are bringing forward in time a campaign of exploration that the oil companies left to themselves would not yet attempt. This and the straightforward economy of a joint effort are adequate justification for this venture, although it has little political significance and is much more a classical piece of international co-operation than a supranational action.

5. COMMUNITY ACTION

The line between co-operation or co-ordination of policies and Community action is not well defined. Community action can be taken to be anything that detracts from national sovereignty; it might be a Community purchasing organization for oil, an allocation system for oil supplies in times of crisis, or joint finance of projects.

In the future there may be funds available raised by the Community on the security of a Community guarantee fund composed of contributions from member states. These would mostly be for Community exploration in oil, but investment in nuclear power could follow the same principle. It has been proposed that Euratom should raise money in the international capital market and use it to finance nuclear power stations in member states. Already the European Investment Bank (EIB) raises money on international markets and lends it for projects which will benefit the Community as a whole or declining regions of the Community or, in some cases, countries outside the Community.

Since 1967 the EIB has met all requests made to it for finance for nuclear plant; it has supported 13 projects to a total of 475 million units of account and would like to assume responsibility for all Community financing of nuclear power. Officials of the EIB argue that there is no need for Euratom to get involved in financial matters where it has no expertise. The objections of the EIB have not apparently been effective and if a Community fund is established it will probably be under the control of Euratom. Nevertheless, the intra-executive power struggle must have consumed considerable effort that would have been better directed to pushing the proposals through.

The interesting question arises, what call will the Community have on coal, oil, gas or nuclear power financed in this way. Germany, France and Italy believe that if there is to be common financing then there must be attached responsibility to the Community. The point is most often made in the form that the United Kingdom is best endowed with indigenous resources, but is lacking in capital. If capital is provided from or by the Community then oil production should be increased to benefit the other member states.

The other particular matter of importance which involves a strong sense of Community is the allocation of oil supplies in times of crisis. In general, a Community response to a restriction of supply could avoid some of the worst consequences, but there are three reservations:

(a) some countries with considerable indigenous resources can only lose, and their co-operation should be recompensed;

(b) technical integration can only create the opportunities; it takes political will to carry them out, and this has been lacking in the Community, as for example in the treatment of the Dutch in November/December 1973;

(c) Community agreements must be fitted into international agreements even if they are viewed with some doubt. Ideally the Community should be a unit within the IEA, but this is not possible while France is not a member.

In fact a majority (10 members) of the Commission considered it legally impossible for eight members of the Community and not France to join the IEA. There was no way of persuading France to join, and the United Kingdom and Germany were determined to go along with the U.S.A.; eventually, to avoid overt conflict, the Commission decided that it was better for the eight to join the Agency, but that all decisions agreed by the eight within the IEA should be compatible with the Common Market. Essentially this procedure institutionalizes a schism in the Community, but it was the only practical solution. Since then a great deal of ingenuity has gone into devising an allocation scheme for the Community which is consistent with IEA requirements and does not involve France in oil sharing. The current Commission proposal is that in times of trouble all member states should be obliged to reduce consumption to the same level, to be decided by the Council, sufficient to ensure obligations are met within the IEA. The oil released would go into a pool along with the stocks of all member states. Embargoed countries would receive an allocation, except France – France is apparently prepared to accept the regime of restrictions. If, therefore, all countries were embargoed except France, then she would receive her normal supply from the producers, but would be obliged to reduce consumption for the benefit of the others. The system of allocation would be operated by the oil companies in accordance with the strategy laid down by member states. The Commission was much criticized after the 1973 crisis; it had foreseen the inevitability of supply problems, but had not worked out a response. The present proposals anticipate a similar situation and provide a premeditated response. It is, however, a fragile arrangement compared to the security that would be provided by a Community purchasing agency.

6. NORTH SEA OIL

There has been much controversy about what influence the oil companies, the U.K. Government and the Community has, or should have, over the control of the depletion of North Sea petroleum reserves and the disposal of the products. In order to determine clearly the consequences of the U.K. being a member of the Community, it is helpful to compare the situations where the U.K. is outside the Community and develops a national policy and where the U.K. is in the Common Market. In theory there is a difference because the U.K. could restrict exports and sell oil internally at a low price to maximize the benefits to the U.K. economy in general, in the way that the U.S.A. have done with their indigenous resources. To some extent the U.K. has done this with natural gas, using the British Gas Corporation's monopoly purchasing right as the instrument. The choice of this strategy for natural gas was determined in large part by the need rapidly to penetrate new markets; this consideration does not apply to oil. It appears that internal sale at low price was never seriously considered by the U.K. Government; the attraction of all that revenue to a government with a chronic public account deficit was too great.

Being in the Common Market makes a low price strategy impossible, unless the U.K. were prepared to make oil available on the same terms to her Community partners and thereby use the resource to the greater benefit of Community industry in general – evidently this is unlikely. Therefore, in practice, there is little difference between the strategy consequential to being in the Common Market and that which the U.K. Government would have chosen anyway. The primary decision – whether to take the profit on the oil or from downstream industrial benefits – is unaltered by membership of the Common Market; secondary decisions on refining policy and depletion policy are to some extent susceptible to Community influence.

Refining Policy: The U.K. will soon be numerically self-sufficient in oil, but although some North Sea oil is technically suitable for U.K. refineries, in other cases the refineries designed for Middle Eastern crude have a capacity reduced by up to 40 per cent, because certain sections of the distillation columns overload when light North Sea oil is used as a feedstock.

The U.K. has three broad options:

(a) refine and use the greater part of North Sea oil here regardless, building more refinery capacity if necessary;

(b) build suitable refineries in the U.K. for North Sea oil, continue to import Middle Eastern oil and sell the light product surplus into Europe;

(c) continue to import significant amounts of Middle Eastern oil and send North Sea oil to Europe for refining.

Intermediate policies are also possible.

Option (c) earns the U.K. foreign exchange equivalent to the freight charge to the Middle East and a low sulphur premium. Option (b) gains in addition the added value of refining, but is logistically inferior and involves extra risk.

There is no doubt that a European government designing a refining policy for the nine member states together would choose option (c) in order to avoid depressing the refining industry in continental Europe and in order to minimize transport costs in general and transport of refined products across the North Sea in particular. The most significant obstacles to this rational policy are the U.K. balance of payments and its desire to preserve security of supply. The optimum European refining policy loses the U.K. the added foreign exchange value of refining. Self-evidently it also reduces the U.K. security of supply because whatever allocation systems may be agreed in principle, when the crisis comes the inertia of established patterns of trade will be important, and therefore countries with indigenous supplies will benefit.

Representatives of the U.K. Government and national civil servants have recently claimed that the U.K. will refine at home a large proportion, two-thirds is often mentioned, of her North Sea oil. The attitude of the Commission is that the U.K. can do what it likes providing that it does not infringe Article 34 of the Treaty of Rome, which forbids quantitative restrictions on trade between member states. If, therefore, another member state were prepared to pay more for North Sea crude than U.K. refineries, and if the crude were available, then the U.K. would be obliged to let it go. Application of Article 34 could certainly prevent the U.K. carrying out its stated refining policy because the depressed refining industry in Europe could afford to calculate a refining cost related to short-term marginal costs without any component to represent the capital cost of refining; the overloaded U.K. refining industry would have to calculate a long-term marginal cost including a capital charge; this difference plus a cost advantage in transport would certainly draw the crude to European refineries in the absence of quantitative restrictions imposed by the U.K. Government.

The Commission views this conflict between the Treaty and U.K. pretensions as an effect not so much of U.K. intransigence as of the absence of any intelligent U.K. refining and depletion policy for the North Sea. It is sanguine about the consequences for refining because it believes that Article 34 plus the resistance of the oil companies to building more refineries in the U.K, and adopting a non optimum strategy will be sufficient to force the U.K. to a European solution. In fact little is really at stake for the U.K.; a large refinery brings about 40 jobs and the value added is only 4–6 per cent of the final cost of oil to European states.

It appears, then, that the Commission is largely relying on the companies to do the job for them by refusing to build refineries and by arguing the European case – although in the last resort the companies could go to the Commission. Oil companies have no European ideals, but they know there is commercial gain in optimizing European operations as a whole. They are not perfect Europeans, because they optimize within their international framework according to their own objectives, but tactically in this matter they are powerful allies. In practice, it may be wise for the Commission not to interfere and to let the oil companies handle the problem, but philosophically it is one more example of how the responsibility for a European policy for oil has been left to the companies, and the Commission has abandoned the initiative.

Depletion Policy: The greatest controversy over North Sea oil and the Community has been reserved for the question of who owns the oil and who has the right to determine the rate at which oil can be extracted. The Commission's stance has been decidedly contradictory. One of the famous 46 points in October 1972[14] was: to substitute for gas extracted in the Community a Community right of pre-emption for the existing national rights of pre-emption. The preceding month M. Spaak had said, in London: 'We believe it would be in the interest of the Community as a whole ... that if pre-emption rights are to exist ... they should be in favour of the Community rather than of any national state'.[15]

The prevailing view in the Commission now appears to be that depletion policy is clearly the responsibility of the British Government, providing they observe Article 34 of the Treaty of Rome. The Commission has presumably adopted this view, and now expresses it strongly, to placate the U.K. Government. On the other hand there are inconsistencies in the treatment of different marine resources. Fish appear to be a resource with some Community rights of pre-emption; if the fishing policy is agreed then the different treatment of oil and fish will be striking. It may be that the suggestion of a Community right of pre-emption to other marine resources will come up again sometime.

In passing, one might note that the powers taken by the U.K. Government in order to control the depletion of the North Sea province are powers to cut back production and delay the start of production in existing fields. The consequence is to reduce the cash flow of companies and government, and therefore the profitability of the investment. It would be altogether much better for the government to calculate the production profile that it wanted to see from the North Sea and then to delay investment if production prospects exceeded future requirements. This procedure requires a clearer idea of how rapidly the North Sea province should be depleted than the U.K. Government yet has; the procedure adopted is more flexible, although more costly, and suits indecision.

D. Coal

There is not thought to be much opportunity for increasing the use of coal in the Community at present prices or even much higher prices. There are said to be a variety of obstacles to increasing the use of coal.

Electricity suppliers are reluctant to take coal on principle; they much prefer nuclear stations. In theory most electricity producers are self-financing, but in practice most have governments more or less solidly behind them; someone else therefore buys the plant and the high capital cost of nuclear investment does not weigh as heavily in the balance as it might otherwise. Once an electricity supplier has got the plant then it is master of the show; there are far fewer problems and those are technical and are felt to be more under control. This view was strongly reinforced by the action of the miners in the U.K. in 1973/74, when they took advantage of the opportunity offered by the difficulties in oil supply to press their own interests. Regardless of the justice or otherwise of the miners' case, there is little doubt but that the sight of the coal industry exploiting the aggression of foreign states for its own ends was disastrous for the long term future of coal in Europe. The Commission has, for example, looked into the possibility of selling coal from the north-east coast of the U.K. to Hamburg where there is a traditional market; the German importers replied that British coal was not only uncompetitive (which the Commission could do something about), but fundamentally was not considered a secure source of supply.

In general, Community coal is still relatively costly, with the exception of lignite, and it is hopeless to try to sell the idea of costly, insecure Community coal to countries without their own coal mining industries.

It seems strange that the enormous rise in oil prices has not made much more European coal competitive. In 1957 production of coal in the ECSC was 290 million tonnes per annum and it was planned to extend production by another 30 million tonnes; production in the same six countries is now 115 million tonnes per annum. Production in the

U.K. was 227 million tonnes in 1957 and is now 120 million tonnes. Since 1957 the rapid adoption of mechanized procedures, especially power loading and self-advancing supports, has much increased the productivity of labour, and crude oil costs in real terms have risen. Where, one might ask, has all the coal gone? The explanation lies mainly in the profound change in the structure of energy use. Since 1957 the use of light refined oil products has increased much faster than the demand for energy in general or crude oil in particular. In the refining process some fuel oil is always produced and must be disposed of in the same market for bulk energy as coal. Fuel oil, therefore, is always sold 10 per cent cheaper than coal, and now there is much more of it than in 1957. Also since 1957, the demands of working men have gone up; in general, they are better paid now in real terms, and in particular a higher differential is required to attract men into the dangerous and unpleasant job of mining.

There is a strong belief in the Commission that imports of coal could play a larger part in Community energy supply. One recommendation of the New Energy Strategy[1] was:

... the conclusion of long-term contracts and the participation by Community industry in joint-venture mining operations in non-Member countries should be encouraged. The Community market should therefore be open to imports ... a true joint trade policy should gradually be implemented.

This idea is always proposed *sotto voce* because of the great political power of the coal mining unions in Germany and the United Kingdom. Imported coal in the past has not been a reliable source of supply because the price has tended to fluctuate; when not needed it was cheap, when needed it was expensive. This is not unreasonable. It is now believed that coal could be imported at a reasonable price from Australia, Poland, Canada and South America if the Community were prepared to accept long-term contracts and participate in the financing of the development.

Much of the coal that could be imported to Europe lies in remote areas requiring risk capital for exploration. Exploitation of any find would require enormous expenditure on infrastructure before the mine was even begun. Townships for the workforce, schools, hospitals, road and rail communications, bridges and ports would be required to support the operation and European governments would have to pledge some political support if host governments sought to renegotiate the terms of their participation at a later stage of the operation.

There are powerful interests operating against world traded coal and few in its favour. The mining unions are implacably opposed to it; national organizations like the National Coal Board identify their interests with indigenous production almost as completely as do the unions; of the big users the electricity supply authorities have some experience of coal imports, but now prefer nuclear stations; there are no entrepreneurial exploration, transport and trading companies working with coal as oil companies work with oil to lobby against the established interests. With powerful forces against and little support, imports of coal might not develop even though they were commercially justified.

The most likely power to develop behind world traded coal is the oil companies. For a long time they have been thinking about how to start adapting to a future where the volume of trade in oil would cease to support their present size or to fulfil their future objectives for growth. They have assessed the potential of coal and nuclear energy as alternative outlets for their talents, expertise and financial resources. Initially, they appeared to prefer nuclear power, but the attempts by Gulf and Shell to market a Gas-Cooled High-Temperature Reactor were a financial disaster. The reprocessing of irradiated fuel elements has been shown to be difficult, risky and unprofitable; in the U.S.A. where private enterprise has been encouraged to take part in the business there has been little enthusiasm either in the oil companies or elsewhere. Consequently, the oil companies have turned to coal. BP has just bought a large interest in the Australian coal mining industry, to add to its existing interest in a U.S. mine; it is exploring in Colombia, Canada, South Africa and Indonesia. Shell International Petroleum is also planning to develop reserves in Australia in association with mining industries; it is also exploring for coal in Indonesia, South Africa, Swaziland and the U.S.A. Some U.S. oil companies are firmly established in coal trading; Continental Oil has 14 billion tonnes of coal reserves in the U.S.A., from which it presently produces 50 million tonnes per year, putting it almost in the same league as the NCB as a coal mining organization. Most other large American oil companies also have coal mining interests.

Shell and BP are said to be interested in European markets and to believe that demand for imports in Europe could be as much as 120 million tonnes a year by 1985. This compares with the estimate by the Community of 35–40 million tonnes by the same date. But the international coal trade will only develop if some political power in Europe can be convinced of the value of coal as an energy source and will give active and sustained support to the concept. European governments either have their own resources (Germany and the United Kingdom) and are inhibited by domestic opinion or have no resources (France) and regard coal as *passé*. There is some evidence that France may be changing her mind; in 1975 Shell shipped a small quantity of coal from South Africa to France, the first substantial international coal trading operation by an oil company.

All too often, internationally traded coal is regarded as an entirely new development and it is forgotten that it is not all that long ago that coal was the largest item of world trade. The pattern of trade was quite different from what might be expected of modern times – then the market was dominated by a single European producer, the United Kingdom. In 1913, for example, coal exports from the United Kingdom reached 98 million tons; they represented 85 per cent of all world trade in coal and included 6 million tons to Russia, 9 million to Germany, 13 million to France, 10 million to Italy, 4 million to the Argentine, 2 million to Brazil and even small quantities to China, Japan, Canada and the U.S.A. There were few countries in the world to whom the United Kingdom did not export coal. Trade resumed after the First World War, reached a peak in the early 1920s and thereafter fell. This piece of nostalgia serves to show, firstly that world trade in coal is feasible, especially with modern developments in solids handling and freight, and secondly that trading patterns can alter slowly, but radically, as circumstances change. The Commission has a great opportunity for initiative; for once it could employ its political sensitivity not to detect the line of least resistance, but to introduce this justified but unpopular policy into the European conscience against the resistance of powerful domestic interests. It should make and publish detailed investigations into the availability of coal in third countries. It should investigate the possibility of joint ventures between the Community, the producing countries and mining organizations or oil companies, and emphasize the role of existing coal mining and coal processing expertise in new ventures dependent on foreign reserves.

The last important element in the perception of the future of coal by the Commission is that coal can only be sold for electricity generation, and here the market has been pre-empted by nuclear power. There is little support for the idea that gasifying coal to synthetic natural gas or liquefying it could be a useful part of European energy supply.

E. Indicative Planning

In order to put into an appropriate context the attempts of the Commission to design a common energy policy, it is necessary to digress on the different intellectual concepts of policy between the U.K. and the continent, particularly the *Étatiste* tradition in France.

Andrew Schonfield[16] writes:

> The essential French view, which goes back to well before the Revolution of 1789, is that the effective conduct of a nation's economic life must depend on the concentration of power in the hands of a small number of exceptionally able people, exercising foresight and judgement of a kind

not possessed by the average successful man of business. The long view and the wide experience, systematically analysed by persons of authority, are the intellectual foundations of the system.

French planning procedures at first sight conflict with the free-market principles of the Economic Community. The French refused to abandon. their planning procedures when the Common Market was formed, but instead set about introducing some form of planning to the Community so that their own measures would not be seen as distortions of competition. After a running battle with the Germans from the first days of the Economic Community,[17] the French finally succeeded in their efforts and the Commission produced a scheme for a medium-term economic policy (the *Projet de Programme*[18]). This was in no sense a plan for the Community, as the plans of the *Commissariat du Plan* were for France, but was simply a guide to avoid conflict between the policies of member states. For indicative planning and the setting of targets for industry to have any practical significance requires that the planners have the means to cajole, bully or threaten industry to comply. To some extent this is the case in France, but the Commission possesses no such power.

The *Projet de Programme* was the first timid venture and neither contained any target for specific industries nor made any effort to obtain powers of intervention. Gradually targets and powers have appeared as proposals in different sectorial policies.

The 1968 guidelines for an energy policy set out the arguments for intervention and proposed powers of invention for the Commission. Much effort thereafter was directed to obtaining the information on prices, trade and investment on which successful intervention could be designed and based. The 1972/73 initiative, as originally drafted, proposed an agency financed by a levy on energy to supervise and intervene in the energy market. The 1975 initiative proposes, for each sector of energy supply, targets which are in some cases supported by analysis of the capacity of the individuals firms in the Community capable of the work required and indications of how that capacity might be deployed to meet the targets, and how gaps in the capacity might be filled.[9] All the trappings of an indicative plan are there, but without the powers to give it practical significance. The Commission undoubtedly would like to acquire the necessary powers, but it recognizes that in the present political climate it is not likely to obtain the consent of member states. Its purpose in designing indicative plans which it is powerless to prosecute is to provide a reference design for Europe's future that all other interested parties can discuss, and in so doing learn more about possibilities and constraints. For example, when the Commission published its objectives it was quickly told that the money was not available; it therefore undertook a detailed examination of finance for energy which has improved the understanding in the Community of the constraints which finance imposes on energy policy. The U.K. cannot have a similar understanding of its own situation, it is argued, because it has not got objectives and therefore cannot cost them. At another level, the objectives permit users and suppliers to plan together; the Commission cannot control what they do, but it can try to provide from its superior vantage point a sketch of the entire scene into which states and companies can fit their own plans.

The intellectual attitude implicit in indicative planning will in itself change the diagnosis of the energy sector and the nature of the policy proposed. An option with the characteristics of nuclear energy will be preferred over one with the characteristics of coal mining. Planning nuclear developments can be done in co-operation with a few large industries with fairly predictable objectives and behaviour. Planning for the coal industry is likely to be affected by the unpredictable objectives and decisions of the labour force and would be much more susceptible to political disturbance. A strategy based on indigenous resources, such as nuclear power, will be preferred to one based on buying imports with the products of diverse manufacturing industries.

It can be argued that the key to success in overcoming all the obstacles to a rapid development of nuclear energy is confidence. If the manufacturers of nuclear plant are confident that the planned programmes will materialize then they will go ahead and invest in manufacturing plant; if the utilities are confident that demand for electricity will rise as forecast they will order new stations; if the suppliers and enrichers of uranium are confident that the demand for uranium will rise as forecast then they will go ahead and explore, and enrichment capacity will be built; if users of electricity are confident that the price of electricity will not be so much higher than that of other sources of energy as to affect the greater convenience and efficiency of electricity then they will go ahead and invest in equipment using electricity, so creating the demand and closing the cycle. Odds and ends such as reprocessing and waste disposal can be dealt with in a more leisurely fashion, as they are not essential to the successful functioning of the cycle. If confidence prevails then the programme may be possible, but without confidence little may happen. In these circumstances the opportunities for 'a small number of exceptionally able people, exercising foresight and judgement of a kind not possessed by the average successful man of business' are obvious. 'The long view and the wide experience, systematically analysed by persons of authority' are crucial if the programme is to succeed.

Whatever the merits of indicative planning and U.K. pragmatism, the existence of different intellectual traditions partly explains why EEC energy policy has been met in the U.K. by hostility verging on disbelief.

References

1. *Towards a New Energy Policy Strategy for the European Community* (*Bulletin of the European Communities, Supplement 4/74*).
2. *Community Energy Policy Objectives 1985, Com(74)1960* (Brussels, 1974).
3. *Community Action Programme on the Rational Use of Energy, Com(74)1950* (Brussels, 1974).
4. *Medium term guidelines for the electricity sector, Com(74)1970* (Brussels, 1974).
5. *Community Policy in the Hydrocarbons Sector, Com(74)1961* (Brussels, 1974).
6. *Towards a Community Nuclear Fuel Supply Policy, Com(74)1963* (Brussels, 1974).
7. *Support to Common Projects for Hydrocarbon Exploration, Com(74)1962* (Brussels, 1974).
8. *Measures to be taken in the event of oil supply difficulties, Com(74)1964* (Brussels, 1974).
9. *Situation and Prospects of the Industries Producing Heavy Electrical Engineering and Nuclear Equipment for Electricity Generating in the Community* (Working Paper of the Commission, July 1975).
10. *Community Financing of Energy Policy* (Brussels, 1975).
11. *Second Illustrative Nuclear Programme for the Community* (Commission of the European Communities, Brussels, July 1972).
12. *Second Report on Competition Policy* (Brussels, April 1973).
13. *Third Report on Competition Policy* (Brussels, May 1974).
14. *Progrès nécessaires de la politique énergétique communautaire, Com(72)1200* (Brussels, October 1972).
15. *North Sea Conference* (September 1972, sponsored by the *Financial Times*, the *Petroleum Times* and *Investors Chronicle*).
16. Andrew Schonfield, *Modern Capitalism* (OUP, London, 1965).
17. G. Denton, M. Forsyth, M. MacLennan, *Economic Planning and Policies in Britain, France and Germany* (Allen and Unwin).
18. *Projet de Programme de Politique à Moyen Terme, 1966–70 Com(66)170* (Brussels, April 1966).

IV

Appraisal of Policy

A. The Inertia of the Initial Vision

The percept of M. Monnet and others that economic integration in the ECSC, the EEC and Euratom would induce political union, required above all else change. It required that the organization of the economy change so that as a natural consequence of that change existing institutions would lose their sway, and the influence of the Community could pervade the new order. The Community would provide technical solutions to the problems thrown up by the process of change; affinities, interests, alliances would be created inevitably and irreversibly within Europe. Gradually people would form expectations of the Community and perceive their interests in its polity.

For this idea to work, the quality and rate of change had to be anticipated in the policies and powers of the Community. The structure of Community institutions and the attitudes of the people in them could hardly have been worse adapted to the changes in energy supply that were to come, indeed that had already started.

Curiously, nuclear energy was considered the prime example of the theory; the absence of any vested interests in nuclear power and the opportunities which this gave to the Community institutions were explicitly noted in the report of the Spaak Committee. Nuclear energy was to cause the renaissance of Europe and Euratom was to be the midwife. By no other enterprise was the Commission to be so invested with authority as by its leadership in the nuclear age.

In our cynical times, it is said that Euratom was never really conceived in those terms, but was dressed up to look important for political reasons. There is certainly evidence that this is an accurate picture of the opinions of national governments; their attitudes are examined in the first chapter of this book. But what is certain is that the vision was genuinely shared by many of those who designed the Communities and who shaped their early energy policy.

In any case, whatever the real extent of the enthusiasm for nuclear power, the institutions were designed and energy policy formulated as if it were real, and that is all that matters for this purpose.

It is ironic that the very year in which the *Target for Euratom* was published and in which the Rome Treaties were signed, should indeed have been a turning point in energy supply. But it was a change that the Commission was simply unable to exploit. The three Executives of the Community responded in different ways. For the High Authority of the ECSC it brought a never ending series of problems; the Executive had to alleviate unemployment, co-ordinate protection, mediate and disguise conflict. For Euratom it complicated the advocacy of nuclear power; the Executive was forced to base its case on the future.[1] For both the ECSC and Euratom the response to change was to defend the status quo, in one case real, in the other ideal. The EEC was responsible for oil, along with natural gas, hydroelectric power and electricity, but the Commission's principal concern was building a customs union and it had little time for a sector which apparently was well able to look after itself.

The attempts to form a common energy policy within the Inter-Executive Working Group were without exception responses to change. At no time did the Community seek to direct that change to further the cause of European integration. Even before the Rome Treaties were signed the initiative in energy policy had passed to the oil companies; that is not to say that they controlled energy policy, but they initiated change; the Commission and national governments responded.

And what an excellent European job the companies did. The companies consistently provided the right quantities and qualities of products from their international resources. They planned port facilities, refineries, storage, pipelines and distribution networks, with as little concern as possible for national boundaries. The oil companies therefore possessed in practice both the initiative and the European vision which in principle were the prerogative of the Community executives.

Although the rapid development of new European oil supply policies by the oil companies was undoubtedly a result principally of new and improved technology in tankers, pipelines and refineries, along with the growth of demand for oil products, it is probable that the movement towards political integration did help to some extent. The removal of barriers to trade between Community countries and the simplification of procedures for the movement of goods across frontiers probably assisted and modified a development that would in any case have been irresistible. Some credit for the technical excellence of the solution must therefore go to Commission initiatives. But the point is that in no way did this imperceptible success augment the prestige of the Commission or embellish the concept of European unity.

Oil played almost verbatim the role written for nuclear energy; it provided Europe with cheaper energy than the U.S.A. and it revitalized European industry. It is argued in the first chapter of this book that even at the time of the *Relance* Committee a dispassionate look at the world would, and did, see that oil was going to be the principal energy source in Europe. The Oil Committee of the ECE without making detailed forecasts of the future identified the probable direction of change. If European institutions had been designed to cope with this change then the Commission might have been more effective. An oil supply agency similar to the Euratom supply agency could have been set up with a right of option over the oil and natural gas produced in the Community and the exclusive right to conclude contracts for the supplies of oil and natural gas coming from outside the Community. A common market in oil products could have been established much more easily at that stage. Control by national governments, present in some countries even then, was on the whole weaker than now. By the time the Executives were merged and the Commission had set about constructing an interventionist policy for oil and natural gas, the companies and national governments were deeply entrenched.

We now have a situation in which the Commission with its right hand (the Directorate-General for Competition), investigates the behaviour of the oil companies for unfair practices during the oil crisis,[2] and with its left hand (the Directorate-General for Energy) hands them the unwanted responsibility for organizing an allocation system. In general, the Commission frequently hands over to the oil companies effective responsibility for finding a European solution: for a European supply policy in the 1960s, for an allocation system in 1973/74, and for driving the U.K. into a rational refining and depletion policy in the 1980s.

The first legacy from the initial vision is, then, an absence of Community influence and a presence of distinct national differences in the most important energy sector of the present time. The second legacy is the presence in the Commission of able and enthusiastic advocates of nuclear power, with comparatively little responsibility for real events, and a responsibility for nuclear matters as a whole that is much less than was anticipated; they make up a persistent lobby in the Commission for nuclear energy. The influence of this lobby fluctuates, but is strongest after each Middle Eastern crisis. When the Commission made the political decision to design an energy policy that would reduce imports of oil, the nuclear club had no need to prepare plans because they were ready. The permanent presence of this unsatisfied lobby within the Commission pre-empts the investigation of alternatives.

The third legacy afflicts not just the European Community but the whole world. The enormous investment that has been made in nuclear energy since 1957, including the military investment, prejudices the future. The investment comprises not only capital, but also careers and prestige. The continuing need, as it is thought, to continue with a military nuclear programme also evidently eases along the commercial programme by sharing some of the costs. If the modern circumstances had been clearly perceived in 1957, then perhaps different energy sources would have been preferred, but it was not, and the errors of the past commit us to nuclear energy in the future.

Basically, this argument is a simple matter of sunk costs and as such is susceptible to analysis, but psychologically, sunk costs tend to carry more weight than is economically justified and this is exacerbated in the European Community by the particularly strong identification of nuclear and European ideals.

B. Energy Carriers in Europe – Electricity, Tankers or SNG?

The whole of Community energy policy rests firmly on the assumption that demand for electricity will grow rapidly, and electricity will become the principal carrier of energy in Europe. The proposals for nuclear power are predicated on the forecasts of electricity demand; the limited future for coal is predicated on the grounds that it can only be sold for electricity generation, a market which has been pre-empted by nuclear energy; the refusal to think clearly about cost and security is disguised by the assertion that the nuclear capacity will only be meeting an exogenous rise in electricity demand and will therefore be competitive.

It is clear now that the nuclear capacity built in Europe by 1985 will be much less than the 200 GW(e) recommended by the Commission, and probably less than 100 GW(e). Nevertheless, the belief still prevails that the only fundamental changes in the structure of energy supply within Europe that are possible or desirable are those associated with nuclear energy; the development of the infrastructure of energy transmission and distribution should be strongly biased to electricity and the use of electricity should be encouraged.

The assertion is based on arguments roughly classified into two groups: broad political arguments and extrapolation of present economic trends. In broad political terms nuclear energy is seen as a secure source of supply; it is justified by that alone and the thrust of the argument is simply that uses for electricy must be found and its penetration of the market contrived. The second group of arguments depends on extrapolation of past increases in the consumption of electricity and the prevailing economic trends to install nuclear plant and retreat from coal.

Neither group of arguments is satisfactory. The economic argument should be presented in terms of the cost in final use in 1985, and broad political judgements should at least be made in full knowledge of the financial penalties incurred, which can only be known from an analysis of costs in final use.

The forecasts of electricity demand on which proposals are based are as follows:

	1980	1985	1990	2000
Total electricity produced (TWhr)	1,540	2,400	3,650	6,800
Total generating capacity (GW(e))	390	540	750	—
Total nuclear capacity (GW(e))	67	200	400	1,000

Figures for installed generating capacity and the nuclear component are also given; they are all taken from the *Medium-Term Guidelines for the Electricity Sector*;[3] they are less than the figures in the New Strategy,[4] but greater than those agreed by the Council of Ministers.

If the figures for total electricity generating capacity and total electricity produced are assumed to be true, then the proposals for nuclear energy follow logically, albeit only on an optimistic assumption of nuclear costs. But it is not clear how these former figures are obtained; in another document about Community nuclear fuel supply policy,[5] it is said that:

> Close analyses of the potential expansion of electricity production, which is the preferred way of exploiting nuclear energy, gives some idea of the future market for nuclear electricity; such an analysis has been made in *Medium Term Guidlines for the Electricity Sector, Com(74)1970*. The target proposed (. . .) is slightly lower than the market potential.

There is, however, no serious analysis in *Com(74)1970* to support this claim; the figures for installed generating capacity and units produced seem to be obtained by exponential extrapolation over long periods at speculative rate constants between 7 and 9 per cent per annum. The task of absorbing the enormous quantities of electricity which it is proposed to generate is assigned to the domestic sector, because it has grown rapidly in the past, and because industry is not expected to reinvest in electrical equipment fast enough to absorb much of the production. Space heating, particularly storage heating, is identified as the main market.[3]

Although cheapness and convenience are stressed as qualities of electricity, no attempt is made to quantify how competitive it will be with other energy sources, and to verify whether it is likely that the market can be penetrated at the rate required. It is usually agreed that electricity can be made more cheaply from nuclear fuel than fossil fuel, providing that the load factor on the generating plant exceeds a certain value which depends on commentator and circumstance. It is also

135

commonplace that off-peak electric heating is not now much dearer than gas or light fuel oil and will get cheaper as more nuclear generating capacity is installed. Observations on the merits of nuclear energy for base load generating and the relative cheapness of storage heating are combined in Commission publications to imply that electricity from nuclear power stations will give cheap space heat, although the argument is never put explicitly.

There are two reasons why this deduction is false. Firstly, nuclear energy is a good source of power because the alternative is to use fuels at a low thermal efficiency (15–40 per cent depending on circumstances). If nuclear energy is to provide electricity for space heat then it is competing with simple combustion of fuel at high thermal efficiency (50–90 per cent). In principle heat could be taken directly from the nuclear reactor, obviating the need for conversion to electricity and our objection would not then hold, but it is difficult to distribute heat raised in this way, and in the short term this will not often be a practical proposition. Secondly, off-peak electricity is now sold at a low price because demand for electricity is less on a winter night than on a winter day, and the marginal cost of off-peak heating is just the operating cost of stations with low operating cost that otherwise would not run at off-peak times. Provision of off-peak electricity therefore does not require the building of extra generating capacity and the marginal cost contains little or no capital cost. If, however, enough storage heating is installed to balance demand throughout the day, then thereafter direct and storage heating must be kept in balance and both contribute to peak demand for electricity. The marginal cost of providing electricity for direct and storage heating is then approximately equal and includes some part of the capital cost of generating plant.

Slightly more than half of the 3,650 TWhr of electricity proposed for 1990 is to be used in homes; this would be, on average, about 19 MWhr per home – almost enough to service an all-electric house. This very rough calculation implies, then, that a large fraction of domestic energy in the Community would be supplied as electricity. In a free market this could happen only if electricity were so much cheaper than alternatives that householders could justify reinvestment in electrical heating equipment.

In fact, it is not difficult to show that because of three factors – the low efficiency with which heat from a nuclear reactor is transported as electricity to space heat in a home, the very high capital cost of nuclear-fuelled electricity generating stations, and the low utilization of the electrical generating equipment built to meet a seasonal heat load – space heat from nuclear electricity is more costly than space heat from distributed oil products under present conditions. Oil prices would have to double or triple to make the electrical alternative break even.[6,7,8]

It is extraordinary that this simple observation is not understood by many of the political and administrative personnel in the Commission. It is current there that nuclear power breaks even with oil when oil reaches $7 a barrel. On an optimistic assessment of nuclear costs, this is true if the two fuels are competing as a source of electricity, not heat, and if the investment is used for a large fraction of the year at full load; these conditions do not apply to space heat, and not much better to industrial process heat. It is difficult, then, to imagine the remarkable market penetration on which the Commission's proposals depend. The competitiveness of electricity is further reduced if the costs of a continued expansion of nuclear power are to be recovered also.

Moreover, in the 1980s when penetration of the domestic space heating market will be crucial, there are likely to be substantial supplies of natural gas from the North Sea and outside the Community, and of light oil products from the North Sea, both of which are suitable for heating at low load factors and easily distributed. Competition for this part of the energy market may be strong, and electricity appears disadvantaged.

Because fossil fuel is converted to electricity at a low thermal efficiency, and because even with a large nuclear programme much of the electricity generated for space heating will come from fossil fuel, the net saving of fossil fuel is not large. In 1990 the proposals for nuclear energy would save about one-quarter to one-third of the fossil fuel that would otherwise have been burnt in boilers for space heat. Of course, the fuel burnt in power stations is usually of lower quality than that distributed to homes, which is some compensation.

The proposals for nuclear power therefore carry a considerable cost penalty, estimated approximately at £5–10,000 million a year for the EEC in reference 7, and something like £10,000 million a year for Western Europe in reference 8.

But the aim of Community energy policy is to reduce oil imports. The extent to which cost should be traded against security has not been consistently thought out in the common policy, but clearly on this basis one could justify some nuclear capacity in excess of the economic optimum. However, there is no reason to prefer the security of nuclear power to the security of solar heating, of more Community coal production, or of still more efficient use of energy; in all cases security is being bought by Community capital and the allocations should be in equilibrium. Similarly, there is no reason why these forms of security should be preferred to the security to be gained by directing consumer expectations to less energy-intensive activities. This reorganization of supply and demand towards equilibrium would substantially reduce the nuclear component and make the policy more manageable in other ways.

But tankers and electricity are not the only vehicles for moving energy. The preferred source of energy for a multitude of tasks is, for those fortunate enough to have the opportunity, natural gas. At the moment natural gas is available rather cheaply out of the ground, but it is possible to synthesize chemically similar material from other fossil fuels. The transport and distribution of energy as natural gas is cheaper than either electricity or oil in tankers and environmentally far superior. It is worth sketching the economics of the process. Again we consider the problem of supplying electricity to meet a large total of electric space heating demand having a pronounced seasonal variation. It is customary in the planning of electricity supply networks to try to optimize the proportions of generating plant of different characteristics. Because of practical constraints and uncertainties it is difficult to know exactly what significance to attribute to a mathematical optimum, but the procedure is a helpful guide. Highly capital-intensive options with low running costs (nuclear stations) are deployed to meet the base load of electricity demand persisting throughout the year; stations of intermediate capital cost and running costs (fossil fuelled steam sets) are deployed to meet a load which only persists for a part of the year; stations of low capital cost and high running cost (gas turbines and inefficient, amortized steam sets) are deployed to meet the peak of demand;[9] the last category generates only a little electricity and is of no great relevance to the present argument. The proportions of the different plants will depend on prevailing capital and operating costs. Under most foreseeable conditions, the bulk of electricity for space heating would be provided by fossil fuel fired steam sets, because the load persists only for part of the year. But fossil fuels can also be converted to substitute natural gas. There is a rule of thumb,[10] accurate enough for this purpose (± 25 per cent), that the capital costs of plant for converting coal to premium fuels (e.g. electricity, SNG, gasoline) are the same per unit of coal input. If we extend this rule to the conversion of heavy fuel oil to premium fuels (i.e. electricity, SNG) and if we take 28 per cent as being the overall efficiency of conversion of fossil fuel to space heat through the vehicle of electricity, including distribution losses, and 56 per cent as being the overall efficiency of conversion of fossil fuel to space heat through the vehicle of SNG,[11] then it is obvious that the SNG is the cheaper route under all conditions, because the capital cost of the conversion plant per unit of energy output is lower for SNG, and the operating cost per unit of useful heat produced at the consumer's appliance is for SNG roughly half that of electricity.

Evidently, if fossil fuel prices were much higher or nuclear costs much lower, then some of the electric space heating load would come from nuclear electricity and the simple calculation described above would not be adequate. More complex calculations show[12] that even if the costs of the nuclear fuel cycle remain what they are now, then the cost of fossil fuel would need to double before the electrical option broke even with the SNG option.

The requirements for industrial process heat cannot be analysed so easily because the sum of loads has considerable diversity and fluctuations tend to cancel out when added together, giving a total load more constant than most of the individual contributions. But even if industrial process heat loads combined to give a perfectly flat total load on the electricity supply system it can be shown[12] that a rise in fossil fuel prices of 50 per cent would be necessary before heat from nuclear electricity broke even with process heat from SNG.

This argument is little affected by the possibility of a rapidly expanding programme of commercial fast reactors. The fast reactor is unlikely to produce electricity at a lower cost than thermal reactors operating on uranium at current prices. At the simplest level this is because a high proportion of the cost of electricity from any nuclear reactor is depreciation of capital; the cost of fuel is a secondary influence. Consequently even if the fuel costs of a fast reactor were zero and it was the same capital cost as a thermal reactor, then the resulting cost of electricity sent out would be only 20–30 per cent lower. In fact, fast reactors will almost certainly have a higher capital cost and the fuel cost may not be much less than for thermal reactors. This latter point can be made simply by the following argument. With present conditions the value of fissile material (plutonium and uranium) recovered from reprocessing, assessed by comparison with present prices for uranium ore, does not quite justify economically the reprocessing operation. It follows that the cost of reprocessing alone will produce an effective fuel cost for the fast reactor somewhere in the region of the current fuel cost for thermal reactors. Fast reactors may well extend the life of recoverable uranium reserves, but they will not produce electricity at any lower cost than thermal reactors now do, and the cost may even be higher.

We have argued that for a wide range of future conditions SNG will service most space heat loads and some industrial process heat loads at lower cost than electricity. The possible sources of SNG are heavy fuel oil, indigenous coal and imported coal. If an effort were made to establish a coal gasification industry, there is little doubt but that it would have to compete with similar processes gasifying heavy fuel oil and that the heavy fuel oil would be available at a competitive price, for the same reasons as cause fuel oil always to be sold at prices which undercut coal for electricity generation.

Indigenous coal is high in cost; there is apparently little scope for increasing indigenous output. Nevertheless, each tonne of the present output of Community coal which is gasified instead of being burnt for electricity will remove the need for one tonne coal equivalent of nuclear energy, and the transfer is commercially justified. The effective role of existing production in the Community energy balance would therefore be extended.

The original Commission target for the EEC in 1990 was that 2,500 TWhr of electricity should be produced from 400 GW(e) of nuclear fuelled generating capacity.[3] The same energy, in thermal content, could be obtained instead by:

(a) transferring 150 million tonnes of heavy fuel oil from power station consumption to gasification; and

(b) transferring 200 million tonnes of coal from power station consumption to gasification; and

(c) importing 200 million tonnes of coal for gasification;

or, of course, many other combinations.

The entire thermal content of the massive nuclear programme to 1990 is equivalent to reorganizing the conversion of some coal and heavy fuel oil and importing 200 million tonnes more coal, or a smaller weight of additional oil.

This conclusion may be difficult to accept because it conflicts with intuition. In Europe now there is a good case for installing more nuclear plant if what is wanted is base load power. There are also mines producing coal at higher cost than imported oil. The short-term economic pressure, therefore, is to install nuclear plant and retreat from coal. Moreover, natural gas from the North Sea and even LNG from distant sources is cheaper than SNG is likely to be from indigenous coal. It seems absurd to advocate making the same commodity more expensively.

If one believes that indigenous oil and gas will be available in large quantities, or if one believes it will be possible to import oil without difficulty or political risk, then it is right to ignore SNG as an energy carrier, but the fashionable perception of the future is that indigenous production and/or imports will be restricted by physical shortage or political constraint so that, at the margin, heat will be supplied from nuclear fuel. In these circumstances SNG appears a better carrier of energy for heat than electricity and fossil fuel a better source than nuclear energy.

It follows that gasification of bulk fuel has at least as bright a commercial future as the next generation of nuclear reactors, and research and development should be funded accordingly. It also follows that the import of large quantities of coal through long-term contracts should be considered seriously for European energy policy, perhaps as a joint venture between the Community, the producing country and appropriate mining organizations.

Finally, it must be said that EEC documents recognize the prospects for gasification, but suggest that it 'is unlikely to lead to substantial demand before the middle of the 1980s, as the required technical processes will not have been perfected until after that period'. This shows more foresight than the U.K., where it does not seem to be accepted, outside the coal industry, that gasification has any prospect worth research and development. What the EEC Commission does not seem to accept is that gasification of coal eventually offers a much cheaper source of security than nuclear electricity for two reasons: firstly, because the technique makes more efficient use of existing coal production – each MTCE gasified releases 2 MTCE from the electricity supply system; and secondly, because SNG as a carrier services heat loads at low load factors at lower marginal cost than electricity. Nuclear capacity built on the scale envisaged might do irreparable damage to the SNG alternative, because it would establish a dominating electricity supply infrastructure, which once built would be run preferentially because of the low operating costs.

C. Cost and Security

The trade off between cost and security has been a constant theme of community policy, identified by the *Relance* Commission on Energy, and made into 'the essential aim of energy policy' by the High Authority in 1964. The choice was declared illusory when the old Commission of the EEC took over the dominant role in energy policy after the merger of the Executives; the doctrine that cost and security did not conflict was preserved in the 46 points. After the oil crisis, security of supply became a still higher priority of a common policy, but the Commission wanted the best of both worlds; it argued that 'the Community must reduce its dependence on others to the utmost extent possible', yet it also required that energy must be available 'at the lowest possible price'. Failure to acknowledge the conflict permitted the Commission to propose a policy far from the economic optimum, predicated on security, but without any discussion how the cost of security was to be assessed. The only people to have faced up to this quandary were the High Authority in 1964; they thought it could be done by giving a price penalty to imports. This would ensure consistency in allocations of capital to supply and use; subsidies to specific projects would not ensure consistency.

In fact the proposition of the High Authority is too simple. Security, like everything else, has a cost, but the costs and benefits of different ways of providing security are difficult to assess, let alone to compare. For example, imported coal provides some security by diversifying sources of supply; it has a social and political cost because of the disturbance to the indigenous mining industry, and if the coal is higher in cost than imported oil it will also have an economic cost. Quotas on oil imports have a cost in that the deficiency in supplies must be made up by more expensive forms of energy. Subsidies to indigenous fuels introduce different inefficiencies and have different costs; energy conservation in excess of the economic optimum carries a cost, as does shifting expectations and activity to less energy-intensive options. Nuclear energy introduces a variety of possible social, environmental, political and economic costs. Doing nothing carries a high political cost. It is, therefore, impossible to express the cost of security in a common measure and treat it simply as an economic input.

Moreover, some forms of security have a low cost, such as diversifying sources of oil supply, but also bring only a small benefit, in this example because most sources are in any case part of OPEC. The problem facing a national government is to choose the most cost-effective measures (within its own conception of what the costs are); the fact that no European government, with the possible exception of France, has adopted measures which carry any real cost can be construed as a *de facto* indication that they value security rather little.

The problem facing the Commission is not only to choose cost-effective measures, but to find measures that appeal to all the member states. It should be clear, however, that progress towards more secure energy supplies can only come from a variety of measures with different effects and is not a simple matter. Generally there are two forms of security: economic stability, i.e. fuel prices which are a reliable guide to investment in energy conservation and alternative sources; and an improved structure of supply, i.e. more energy conservation and more alternative sources. These are discussed in turn.

The member states as individual political entities have quite different interests in the future price of energy. The U.K. being well endowed with secure energy resources of rather high cost (North Sea oil and gas, coal, nuclear power), with production capacity already installed, perceives its interest to lie with high energy prices that protect its own sources. One can argue that even with her own high cost production, if the U.K. can get cheaper energy elsewhere then she would gain by the general benefit to industry. Within its own terms the argument is valid, but in reality the objective of the U.K. is not absolute economic growth, but to do as well as possible in relationship to the Western world, especially the rest of Europe, and to keep the public account deficit in bounds. The immediate U.K. desire for high world energy prices is therefore unquestionable.

The rest of Europe has, by contrast, little indigenous energy; the energy balance for the member states in 1973 is given in the Table on page 144. Their future prospects for truly indigenous production are even grimmer; the production of gas in the Netherlands is expected to peak in 1978 and decline thereafter, and some German coal production is under pressure.

Germany and France have large nuclear programmes, but it will be some time before they deliver appreciable energy. Allowing for the fact that the initial output for base load electricity will be competitive, it will probably not be much before 1985 that the nuclear stations will start producing non-competitive energy. The interest of France, dedicated fiercely to her nuclear programme, is therefore for low world energy prices now and high world energy prices in the future. The interest of the other member states without large nuclear programmes or high cost indigenous energy is presumably in low world prices now and in the future. It is politically impossible, therefore, to agree a level of energy prices all over Europe, at which indigenous energy should be supported. The minimum support price (MSP) for oil at $7 a barrel is an illusion. The only way the U.K. can hope to get a guaranteed high price for its energy production is if it offers the Community something in return.

The only thing the U.K. can offer is security; in return it wants assurances that the energy sector will be a net generator of funds in the future. The bargain could be achieved if the U.K. were to sell parts of its crude oil production into Europe under long-term contracts. The future price could be tied to any number of variables, that is a matter for negotiation, but if the mutual interest exists, and it does, there must be scope for an acceptable bargain. The advantage of this procedure is that it sidesteps the interest in low prices of the other member states, by offering them tangible security now.

The United Kingdom will be forced to sell part of its crude oil into Europe for reasons already sketched; the procedure outlined enables it to do so under the most favourable conditions. The crude oil could well be part of that over which the British National Oil Corporation has an option by virtue of its participation in North Sea production, but for which it has as yet no outlet. Because of the absence of any oil policy in the United Kingdom and because of the perpetual protests that most of the crude will be refined in the United Kingdom against all the evidence, the government of the United Kingdom cannot see where its own interests lie. The Commission might help by publishing an analysis of, and recommendations for, the handling of the North Sea province in a European context, given the existing structure of the European refining industry.

Long-term contracts could also be used to provide some protection for Community coal. This would be more difficult for coal than oil, because it is a less attractive fuel and because if it is transported from the pithead it soon becomes uneconomic. The economic balance

143

Supply of Primary Energy to Member States

Data for 1973

	B	DK	F	G	IL	I	L	NL	UK	Total
Total indigenous	5.7	0.1	39.5	120.7	1.2	24.1	0.0	57.8	116.3	365.3
Solid fuels	5.6	—	17.2	92.0	1.2	0.3	—	1.2	82.8	200.1
Oil	—	0.1	1.9	6.7	—	1.1	—	1.6	0.4	11.8
Natural gas	—	—	6.4	15.3	—	12.8	—	54.8	24.9	114.3
Nuclear energy	—	—	3.3	2.7	—	0.7	—	0.2	7.2	14.1
HEP and others	0.1	—	10.7	40.0	—	9.2	—	—	1.0	25.0
Total imports	43.3	20.6	146.1	149.4	6.1	115.7	5.1	15.9	113.2	613.0
Solid fuels	5.3	2.2	10.1	-10.3	0.5	8.7	2.5	1.7	-1.0	18.7
Oil	30.9	18.4	128.9	145.1	5.6	103.0	1.7	40.2	113.5	588.1
Natural gas	7.3	—	7.7	12.2	—	3.5	0.2	-25.7	0.7	4.1
HEP and others	-0.2	—	-0.6	2.4	—	0.5	0.7	-0.3	—	2.1
Grand total	49.0	20.7	185.6	270.1	7.3	139.8	5.1	73.7	229.5	978.3

Forecasts for 1985

	B	DK	F	G	IL	I	L	NL	UK	Total
Total indigenous	16	n.a.	95	173	3	60	1	71	290	719
Solid fuels	5	—	11	88	2	—	—	—	84	190
Oil	—	n.a.	1	5	—	3	—	2	130	141
Natural gas	—	n.a.	6	19	1	22	—	67	58	173
Nuclear energy	11	n.a.	60	57	—	33	1	2	17	181
HEP and others	—	—	17	4	4	12	—	—	1	34
Total imports	54	n.a.	163	249	9	174	5	27	-2	705
Solid fuels	6	3	19	9	1	15	2	7	2	64
Oil	28	23	113	184	8	140	3	58	-10	547
Natural gas	20	n.a.	31	52	—	19	—	-38	6	90
HEP and others	—	—	4	—	—	—	—	—	—	4
Grand total	70	n.a.	258	422	12	234	6	98	288	1424

Key to countries: B – Belgium; DK – Denmark; F – France; G – Germany; IL – Ireland; I – Italy; L – Luxembourg; NL – Netherlands; UK – United Kingdom.

could be redressed by Community subsidy, but unfortunately coal from the United Kingdom, which is the indigenous source most suitable for expansion, is not regarded on the continent as a secure supply. Little can be done about this in the present system. But if an effective world trade in coal did develop then whatever organization was responsible for fulfilling contracts for export to Europe could perhaps find substitutes for United Kingdom coal when supplies were disturbed, just as the oil industry does at present.

Long-term contracts would reconcile to some extent the conflict of interests of the member states over energy prices. It would do nothing to encourage the development of alternative indigenous sources and investment in conservation. There is one way to do that simply over a broad front, and that is to increase the price of energy. This goes against the immediate interest of the majority of member states, but in fact the overall cost could be low. In appraisal of the viability of alternative sources and of energy conservation procedures, it is often found that the optimum is rather flat, in other words that further investment, although not strictly justified, would incur net losses, after allowing for a reasonable return on capital, that are small compared to the investment itself.

An increase in the price of energy by a tax, the proceeds of which were allocated to alternative forms of energy and conservation, would have a small net cost to Europe as a whole, and would encourage security through conservation. The import duty would be small at first, in order not to overload the fund, and would rise in the future. The funds would be allocated by the Commission to deserving projects, the national allocations being in proportion to the revenue raised from each member. As well as benefiting the security of Europe, the procedure would have great advantages for the Commission, since it would increase its control of real resources. The Commission's control of real resources for energy is small. It can dispose of the levy on the coal and steel industries, and of a direct budgetary allocation for research and development, but in both cases the amounts involved are much smaller than the resources required to shift policy perceptibly. Consequently the only decision open is to choose amongst many deserving cases; the decision which alters policy, that is who to turn away or how far to go, does not arise. In particular, it is difficult practically to influence what will happen in ten years' time.

D. Energy Conservation

Most serious thought in the Commission and most of the pages in its publications are given to the supply of energy rather than to its efficient use. In this the Commission is not unlike other central executive bodies in the member states. To influence energy supply requires intervention in comparatively few types of industry dominated by large concerns; to influence energy use requires intervention in the vast array of energy using activities, private, commercial and domestic. Energy conservation is not an attractive proposition to an administrator.

But the Commission has not completely neglected the subject. Although it has no directorate concerned with conservation it has formed subcommittees on energy conservation, consisting of Commission officers from the existing directorates and of representatives from member states. The subgroups deal with: the thermal insulation of buildings; heating systems; road transport vehicles; transport structures; industrial process heat; power; conversion in power stations; and transformation in refineries.

The interim reports of these subgroups have been published along with draft recommendations to the Council.[13] The reports are compilations of the common currency of where and how energy might be saved, but they miss almost completely the two crucial questions – how much it costs and how it can be enforced. The superficiality of the enterprise is evident in the five concrete recommendations, which the Council approved at its meeting in March 1976:

to promote thermal insulation by publicity campaigns and by the adoption of harmonized standards;

to improve the control of central-heating installations in existing buildings;

to improve driving practice through better information in driving manuals and by defining standards of fuel consumption for vehicles;

to encourage public transport;

better information for the consumer about the consumption of electrically driven appliances.

These are only recommendations and are not binding; their significance can be gauged by the impact in the United Kingdom. But more importantly these recommendations are just a few of the many that anyone with any experience of energy conservation could write down without thought. The difficulty lies not in thinking them up, but in cost and enforcement.

In fairness to the Directorate-General for Energy, the obstacles to a determined campaign of energy conservation are great. The obstacles can be divided into four classes: the inertia of the past, the nature of individual and corporate objectives, the difficulty of legislation and the pervasiveness of energy use. These classes are not exclusive or exhaustive, but they assist a brief discussion.

The inertia of the past comprises all the urban settlements, industrial plant and practice, transport systems and buildings constructed with little thought of the energy required to service them. Large cities require large *per capita* inputs of energy to keep them going, both to carry people, goods and waste in and out of the city, and to distribute and collect them within the city. The growth of private transport is difficult to stop, but consumes much energy. It is more difficult to improve the thermal performance of existing buildings and industrial plant than of a replacement still being designed. Even more pervasive than this legacy of energy-inefficient hardware is the legacy of personal expectations, formulated perhaps as a bigger house further from the city, central heating, a bigger, faster car. These expectations are politically almost irresistible.

The objectives of business are rarely such as to make energy conservation a high priority even, although evidently to a lesser extent, in energy intensive industries. The notion of a businessman ranking the investments open to him in terms of DCF return and choosing all those above a minimum cut-off or choosing the highest returns within a fixed budget – this idea is a fiction. A strong qualitative selection operates; investments that assist survival, increase market shares or develop new products are much preferred to those that save energy. Consequently, whereas public utilities supply energy at a price containing a component to cover capital discounted at 10 per cent or thereabouts, private enterprise will only make investment that uses energy more efficiently if the energy saved justifies the capital invested discounted at 30 per cent, 40 per cent or even 50 per cent. There is, therefore, an enormous discrepancy between the economic criteria for the supply and use of energy.

One solution for government is to legislate for defined standards of energy performance. This is not easy, because the variety of contexts in which energy is used does not permit the simple generalization necessary for legislation. Moreover, legislation can be ineffective or counterproductive. For example, an obligation to insulate walls of buildings heavily could in certain circumstances harm the thermal performance of a building by reducing the solar gain. Moreover, such legislation would do nothing to impede the fashion for designing buildings as radiators, requiring high-capacity air conditioning in summer and disproportionate heating in winter. Some methods for conserving energy are almost outside conceivable legislation; it would be difficult, for example, to force an industrialist to install combined heat and power generation against his will.

There are no easy roads to energy conservation. Price increases have an effect, but often it is limited if the designer or builder of capital equipment does not pay the bill for energy consumption. Experience with grants is not good; if industry is not going to invest, it is unlikely to be tempted by a discount of a few per cent on going interest rates. Legislation is clumsy and difficult to design and enforce. The only answer is to do all these things where appropriate. A possible set of measures in the easier areas is:

insulation standards for all new buildings below a certain size, about the size of a normal house;

thermal performance standards expressed in terms of annual energy consumption per square metre of floor area for all new larger buildings, including factories;

a heavy tax on petrol, which not only restricts consumption of oil as petrol in cars, but reduces the heavy fuel oil to be disposed of and reduces the pressure on the indigenous coal industry;

the provision of grants by the Commission for investment in all forms of energy conservation, including basic research and development of conservation technology; these would be financed by a tax on all fuels, the proceeds from which would be dispensed by the Commission to member states roughly in proportion to the revenue raised from them.

Energy conservation is difficult, but in this aspect of policy the Commission does have one advantage. Individual efforts by member states to conserve energy would impair the competitiveness of that state with its neighbours. Standards achieved in concert would be more acceptable. It would be foolish to insist always on single standards for all Europe. The economically reasonable standards of thermal insulation in southern Italy and in Scotland are not identical. But where one standard is inadequate the form of legislation should be preserved.

In this area the Commission has a great opportunity. Adoption of legislation in concert has the advantages sketched above; moreover, all countries are in favour of conservation, all individual efforts by member states have been unsatisfactory, and no state perceives it as a threat. It is an excellent place for the Commission to push and possibly even to insert the thin end of a wedge in the shape of a Community energy agency. The first essential is to create a Directorate of Energy Conservation with its own staff, rather than to depend on the hard-pressed members of staff in the other Directorates. Energy conservation in the present structure is bound to take second place to officials' primary duty to their Directorate; in some cases there may even be a direct conflict of interest. For example, the combined generation of heat and power which in principle offers one of the largest opportunities for energy saving is dealt with by the staff of the Electricity and Nuclear Directorate. Combined heat and power competes with nuclear power for scarce capital for electricity supply and scarce markets for electricity, but the first priority of the Nuclear Directorate is to insert an enormous nuclear generating capacity into the electricity supply network. There must be a clash of interest, and it is not, perhaps, surprising that in the three years since the Yom Kippur war the Directorate-General for Energy has done nothing at all to advance combined heat and power generation. Most interest in combined heat and power has come from the Directorate-General for Industry, which has commissioned and published an extensive study of what might actually be done and where – far superior to anything that their colleagues directly responsible for energy have produced.[14]

E. The Theory of No Political Will

... the spirit of European understanding shown by the partners of France, who allowed her to determine the course of debate, not only because her representatives were of excellent quality, but also because her favours were worth having.

Lucien de Sainte Lorette
on the EEC Euratom negotiations in 1956.

Everyone is paranoic about the French.

Member of a Commissioner's Cabinet, 1976.

The reason generally favoured by the Commission for the absence of convincing progress in energy policy is a lack of political will from the member states. On the face of it the case since 1968 is certainly strong. The Council waited 11 months to discuss the *First Guidelines*, and then it did nothing substantial despite a series of specific proposals from the Commission; the 46 points and the associated proposals had no greater effect. The Yom Kippur war elicited several affirmations of political resolve, but no decisions of weight; the culprits looked like France, whose conduct was clearly designed to free her foreign policy, and the United Kingdom, whose caprices were a result of uncertainty about her objectives compounded by the desire of certain politicians to strike the right posture at home and a 'Freudian obsession' with North Sea oil. Two sets of factors determine the outcome of the dialogue between the Commission and national interests. There are determinants outside the Commission, the extent of national differences, the intensity with which national administrations pursue their interests, and the value which they put on intangible political unity. There are also determinants comprising the structure, composition and skill of the Commission. To attribute blame to a lack of political will is to emphasize the first set of determinants to the exclusion of the second.

Certainly one might expect the will for a common policy to be frail; there are substantial differences in natural endowments of resources and in the requirements of member states. National administrations will defend their positions strongly because secure energy supplies are seen as strategically important and resources are seen as finite and irreplaceable.

In 1951 a real distinction existed between the coal producing countries: Belgium, France and especially Germany, and the net energy consuming countries: Italy, Luxembourg and the Netherlands. By 1968 all member states were in a similar boat; Germany and the Netherlands still produced substantial quantities of energy, but they, like the others, imported at least one-half of their requirements. Curiously, this equation of poverty did not realize the elusive political will. In fact there had been more progress in previous years, when the Community system of aids to coal mining and the subsidies to coke and coking coal financed by the Community had been wrung out of manifest contrariety. This leads us to what is really an obvious conclusion; differences are necessary to drive the Community. If the situations of member states were identical then there would be no incentive for common policies, because there would be no gain.

It is instructive, to digress, to compare the failure to agree on energy policy with the success in at least agreeing on an agricultural policy.[15] All governments accepted the principle of a common or harmonized agricultural policy. National policies had not maintained farmers' incomes, nor helped modernize farms, nor had they created a logical relationship between national and world markets. Agricultural pressure groups in the Community were prepared to support a common policy which promised to put some of this right; some member states, particularly France and the Netherlands, would support it vigorously in the Council of Ministers, and were prepared to make progress in the common agricultural policy a condition of their co-operation elsewhere. Finally, no one perceived it as a fundamental threat.

But not only did the Commission start from a favourable position, it operated with great skill; its proposals were evidently impartial, expert and commanded respect; it was successful in rallying farmers and other pressure groups and thereby convincing national politicians that their own aspirations would be served by joining the bandwagon; it successfully dramatized its proposals, made them symbolic of the wider aims of integration, and in that way built a broad coalition of support outside specialist agricultural interests. It seems also to have used its mediative function to great effect; Signor Mansholt, the Commissioner responsible from 1958–72, was particularly adept at arranging compromises to drive the CAP along. The Commission was also successful in assuaging fears that the more efficient farmers in the Netherlands and France would drive others out of business without compensation, and in projecting the vision of a common policy in which the long-term benefit to the common good would compensate national short-term sacrifice.

In comparison, in 1968 national energy policies were working well The oil companies had kept the oil flowing during the 1967 Middle East crisis, prices were low and stable, there was no instability in the relationship between national and world markets; there was no obvious benefit in a common policy. There were no interest groups anxious to promote a common policy, with the exception of coal producers and coal miners' unions. No country stood to gain enough from the proposals to press them in the Council of Ministers.

The circumstances in 1968 were not favourable to the evolution of a common policy, and the accusation of a lack of political will (which in some circumstances is quite respectable) does seem reasonably convincing. A necessary, but by no means sufficient, condition for the presence of political will for a common policy is that there is scope for, and that the policy will cause, a redistribution of resources to the benefit of almost everyone; this requires precisely that member states have different endowments. The U.K. has brought to the Community the potential for a common policy, but there is an enormous snag.

A redistribution of a resource to the benefit of all is easiest when the resource satisfies two requirements: it is expanding and renewable. A resource may expand because of a flourishing economy, improving technology, or because the policy will in itself make more available. In the common agricultural policy the countries well endowed with agricultural resources were perfectly content to expand production because they could expect returns indefinitely; similarly the countries with efficient manufacturing industries were content to expand production to meet the increased demand within a customs union.[16] In contrast, many of the resources of the U.K. are either finite or incapable of expansion because they are close to the limit at which they cease to be renewable; the obvious examples are fishing and energy. A country well endowed with fossil fuels will, fashionably, perceive them as finite, and be tempted to conserve them for herself; the simple concept of specialization within a common market will not, therefore, produce the intrinsic driving force for a common policy that has occurred elsewhere.

A common energy policy should, therefore, aim at benefiting from the different strengths of the United Kingdom and other member states. In the Commission this view is generally thought to be only half true. The other half of the picture is supposed to be that France has a nuclear industry and is an important quantity in a common nuclear programme. It is argued that the United Kingdom has a lot to gain from the Community in nuclear power, because the Euratom treaty favours weak nuclear countries, and if the U.K. wants to participate in advanced nuclear technology the Community will help it. Probing reveals that the impression of France as a strong nuclear power is based on the belief that the French nuclear industry is making, or is about to make, money, and the Eurodif enrichment plant is cited as being 90 per cent contracted with severe penalties for default. This impression is significant; it is found not so much among technical people as among the political people and the top administrators. There are two things to say.

Firstly, it shows how effective are French civil servants in projecting favourable perceptions of France within the Community. The U.K. has the advanced gas-cooled reactor which works at higher thermal efficiency, makes better use of uranium and will probably achieve higher load factors than the Light-Water Reactors built by France. The designs of these LWRs are not French; they are built under American licence. The U.K. also has a fast reactor programme essentially as well advanced as the French, although being pressed with less urgency; it had until recently an HTR programme, and it has its own water moderated reactor; it has functioning irradiated oxide fuel reprocessing capacity and an enrichment technique at least the equal of French techniques. It is simply not true that French technology is more advanced than the U.K.'s. Moreover, Germany has a far stronger industrial base than France and, although the U.K. may be weaker than France in the relevant manufacturing industries, it does have under-used capacity which would be of value to a common programme, whereas overloaded French capacity would not.

Secondly, it is true that France is taking risks and in the remote event of her gamble coming off she will be the dominant nuclear power in Europe, but it does little good to France for the Eurodif plant to be 90 per cent contracted with heavy penalties for default if the contracts are with French utilities. But even if France is successful, it is difficult to see how her nuclear programme could be the basis for a common policy; she is not supplying the Community with technology (which is American) or manufacturing capacity. Later she will perhaps provide an expanding resource for other member states, but not now.

In the hydrocarbons sector where the U.K. dominates there is, in contrast, scope for immediate action. The straightforward concept of specialization in a common market is inadequate, we have argued, to provide a motive force for common policy to non-renewable resources; it is necessary to look for more specific complementary needs. The need of Europe is for secure oil; the need of the U.K. is for a guarantee that the energy sector will be a net generator of funds; this could be achieved by long-term contracts for the sale of oil into Europe. The chief obstacle is the U.K. Government's refusal to determine a refining and depletion policy for its offshore reserves which makes allowance for the fact that the U.K. is geographically and constitutionally part of Europe.

The Commission could help the U.K. come to terms with its predicament by making appropriate proposals. Perversely the Commission has begun with proposals which are either of no interest to, or are harmful to, the very state whose support should be harnessed. The U.K. has no interest in Euratom loans for nuclear power stations; it has no interest in Community finance for exploration and production of hydrocarbons, because the oil companies have no difficulty in arranging finance for themselves; any reduction of activity in the North Sea could be offset by concessions in the Petroleum Revenue Tax more easily than by Community loans; the U.K. has no interest in oil sharing without compensation; and it is unenthusiastic about regulating the oil companies, for whom it provides a home. The only measure it has supported in the Council with any enthusiasm is the Minimum Safeguard Price for oil, but that, as we have already argued, is a divisive measure, and unnecessary in a situation where mutual interests can be recognized without difficulty.

Constructive progress towards a common energy policy will depend on identifying matters where there exists a complementary need and where negotiation is possible. The Commission might well begin with its own broad and tentative proposals of how the North Sea province could best be handled in the joint interest of the U.K. and her partners.

F. Proliferation of Thermonuclear Weapons

The proliferation of thermonuclear weapons is an evident threat. In a sense it is the inevitable consequence of the knowledge of how to cause thermonuclear explosions. It would not be realistic to imagine that nuclear weapons will remain the exclusive property of a few nations, given the knowledge and the relentless process by which the advanced technology of today becomes the manufacturing industry of tomorrow. The military consequences of commercial nuclear power programmes are only a modest perturbation in an inevitable evolution. This, at any rate, is the fundamental argument of the French, who are prepared to sell a nuclear fuel reprocessing plant to Pakistan for the quite transparent purpose of countering the military threat from India, although this is denied by both sides. But the facts of the matter are that Pakistan has immense potential for hydroelectric power; it has an embryonic electricity supply network for which nuclear generating capacity is unsuitable because it can only be installed in large amounts and because of its general economic characteristics; it has, at the moment, virtually no nuclear fuel to require reprocessing and in no way can a commercial case be made out for the plant. France is also prepared to supply reprocessing plant to South Africa and was apparently willing to supply a research reactor to Libya. Germany has agreed to supply Brazil with a complete range of sensitive technology – uranium enrichment plant, irradiated fuel reprocessing plant, and heavy water.

153

One cannot discuss proliferation simply as a European problem. The U.S.A. has a chequered record in its contribution to the spread of nuclear weapons. The Government of the U.S.A. has always been more concerned about the proliferation of nuclear weapons than have the governments of Europe, possible because in the last resort it has to deal with the results. The early days of Euratom were influenced to some extent by this American concern; it was the U.S.A. which inspired the non-proliferation treaty (NPT) and, more recently, it was the U.S.A. which put pressure on the European nuclear exporters to sign the London agreement which, although neither binding nor adequate, is at least a beginning. On the other hand the commercial instincts of the U.S.A. have been strong enough to ensure that she made the most of her dominance of the export market for nuclear reactors. Ever since the non-proliferation treaty came into force in 1970 she has persisted in selling reactors and uranium fuel to non-treaty states. For example, in the last weeks of President Nixon's administration, uranium and reactors were offered to Egypt and Israel, two non-treaty states in conflict. President Ford refused to cancel these agreements. More recently the U.S.A. has agreed similar sales to India and Spain. The U.S.A. has always claimed that this does not conflict with her obligations under the treaty. Whether or not this is an acceptable interpretation of the treaty, it would evidently be a much more satisfactory procedure if it were not possible to sell reactors and fuel to states that had not ratified the NPT.

The marketing approach of the U.S.A. has therefore been to sell uranium fuel and reactors, but to refuse to supply either the reprocessing plant, which would make the reactor a source of fissile material, or the enrichment plant. This has in turn influenced the marketing approach of European exporters. France and Germany have agreed to supply reprocessing plant along with reactors as a means of breaking into an otherwise unassailable American market.

For this reason Europe has been, in the past, a serious source of proliferation. The massive nuclear power programmes proposed for Europe and the special relationship assumed with the oil producers ensure that Europe will continue to have a commercial interest in selling nuclear technology in the future. The problem has been exacerbated by the failure of the domestic programmes of nuclear power proposed after the oil crisis and for which the heavy electrical manufacturing and construction industries have to some extent prepared. There has developed considerable over-capacity in the relevant European industries, and the pressure to export is and will continue to be very strong. For example, in Germany the two most important companies are Kraftwerk Union and BBR, the latter being a combination of Babcock and Wilcox and Brown Boveri. These two companies between them have the means to produce about 10,000 MW of nuclear electrical generation capacity a year. The domestic German programme is likely to require about 3–4,000 MW of capacity; the rest must be disposed of abroad. This sort of pressure does not encourage much concern with the morality of nuclear exports. There is, of course, no lack of willing buyers. It is said that Kraftwerk Union's order book for nuclear reactors already amounts to about 30,000 MW. Similarly, over-capacity exists in France, Italy and the United Kingdom.

For various reasons the over-capacity in Italy and the United Kingdom is not an accurate measure of likely exports from these countries. France has persisted with its nuclear programme for longer than other countries, but here as well some revision of plans has directed effort into exports, and this is likely to increase as the forecasts are progressively reduced in size. Effective control of the inevitable proliferation of nuclear technology is essential.

The London agreement is based on four principles; they are that any country which exports nuclear technology must have adequate assurances that the technology will not be employed to make a nuclear explosive of any kind, that the exports will be protected from theft and sabotage, that the technology can only be re-exported under identical restrictions, and that the technology will not be transferred to any plant not subject to the safeguards of the International Atomic Energy Agency.

The effect of the agreement is to ensure that any country which has not signed the Non-Proliferation Treaty (NPT) and which would not therefore normally be subject to IAEA safeguards, but which imports an item from an agreed list of strategically significant pieces of plant or technology, must thereafter submit to IAEA safeguards on that particular item. The rest of the nuclear programme of the recipient stays out of control. Obviously there is no way of verifying that the particular import is not directly or indirectly contributing to a military objective. The system could be greatly improved simply by requiring that thereafter the entire nuclear industry of the recipient be subject to control. It is difficult to see any objection to this extension.

Even so, the success of the agreement would rest solidly on the assumption that IAEA safeguards were adequate. They are obviously not, for two reasons. The safeguards depend on the principle of mass balance, that is that as much plutonium must come out of the reprocessing plant as goes in. But because of losses it is necessary to allow some discrepancy. The figure allowed in the London agreement is not publicly known, but for assessment of the commercial prospects for the fast reactor it is common to use a figure of about 2 per cent. A 1,000 MW reactor would produce about 200–500 kilogrammes of plutonium a year; 2 per cent of that is 4–10 kilogrammes; it takes from five or six kilogrammes to make a nuclear weapon. More seriously, it is virtually impossible to measure how much plutonium goes into a reprocessing plant, because the proportions of plutonium in irradiated fuel elements will depend upon how the fuel element has been used in the reactor and upon the profile and spectrum of the radiation to which it has been exposed. It would be quite feasible to reduce the period of time spent by certain elements in the reactor, thereby achieving a high proportion of the fissile plutonium 239 required for weapons and simultaneously increasing the burn up of other fuel elements to compensate for the reduction in electrical output. In this way weapons grade plutonium could be produced without using a suspicious number of fuel elements to produce the measured electrical output.

There is only one way of really keeping track of plutonium and that is by insisting that all reprocessing of irradiated fuel be done in regional centres under international control and supervision. Diversion of irradiated fuel would then cause a discrepancy in the number of fuel elements used and the number sent for reprocessing. Although science may not be able to measure precisely the plutonium in irradiated fuel elements, there is no doubt about man's ability to count. This procedure would almost certainly reveal any diversion of plutonium. Regional processing plants under international control are favoured by the U.S.A., but opposed by the United Kingdom as being impossible in practice and by the French as being inconvenient.

Although philosophically the root of the evil is knowledge, in practice these measures could greatly reduce the risks. It is quite wrong for France, and to some extent the Community, to abdicate responsibility for their actions on the convenient grounds that it is not 'realistic' to believe that nuclear weapons can for ever be restricted to certain privileged powers.

It is evidently difficult for the Commission to propose harsher restrictions on the sale of nuclear components by European exporters than those imposed by the government of the dominant member of the market, especially when the lax attitude to nuclear exports has developed as a conscious response to American dominance. But there is much that the Commission could do within this constraint. Effective action to restrain the spread of nuclear technology must obviously be international and not just European, but the EEC could participate as a Community and should eventually take the initiative. First, the Commission has to press for Community representation in the matter, to replace the present arrangement whereby Germany, France and the United Kingdom represent themselves. After that it should propose a common policy for exports, to be adopted unilaterally if possible, but much more probably to be pressed in an international forum such as that which produced the London agreement. The eventual aims of a more restrictive agreement should be an embargo on the export of strategically significant technology to any non-treaty country and the development of regional reprocessing plants under international control.

G. The Political Sensitivity of the Commission

There is no power in the Commission to force proposals through against the opposition of member states. We have conceded that for the Commission to succeed in getting member states to adopt its policies, it must demonstrate great skills of political management – understanding, imagination, advocacy and timing. But examination of the political sensitivity of the Commission reveals two possible points of criticism: that in some respects the political objectives have overwhelmed the technical possibilities, and that the Commission's political sensitivity has been used to identify from the outset the line of least resistance.

Euratom was conceived as an institution which would bring enormous political gain, but was predicated on an erroneous appraisal of the technical possibilities. The New Energy Strategy was designed to achieve political aims, to restrict oil imports, to prepare a bargaining position, to exhort. The technical basis was considered secondary and was inadequate.

The old High Authority did not use its political skills to detect the line of least resistance, nor did the Commission of the EEC in the early days. But times changed. In 1964/65 France and Germany made clear the limits to the intervention which they would tolerate; the Executive emerged bruised and less confident, and since then the Commission has rarely opposed the principal political forces forming energy policy in the Community. In 1966 it refused to support German efforts to obtain Community subsidies for the coal industry in the face of opposition from France, Italy and the Netherlands. At the moment it makes no effort to resist the power of indigenous coal producers and mining unions in restricting coal imports to the Community; it makes no effort to influence the development of a sensible European refining policy for North Sea oil because it prefers not to upset the U.K. Government, and finds it politically expedient to leave the job to the oil companies; it refuses to try to raise support for a rigorous policy towards proliferation of nuclear technology because it would face opposition from the U.K. and, especially, from the powerful French nuclear lobby.

In short, the political sensitivity of the Commission has led it to adopt strategies which almost guarantee that energy policy in Europe will evolve in just the same way as if the Commission did not exist.

Political sensitivity should be employed for arranging the adoption of common policies in the face of opposition from member states. This is easily said and terribly difficult to do, but it does seem that the

Commission has shied away from some important problems without a sufficiently sustained effort to find solutions.

References

1. E.g. *2nd General Report* (EAEA, Brussels, 1968), but the formulation of the case for nuclear energy is typical of publications of the period.
2. *Report by the Commission on the Behaviour of the Oil Companies in the Community during the Period from October 1973 to March 1974*, Com(75)675 (Brussels, December 1975).
3. *Medium term guidelines for the electricity sector*, Com(74)1970 (Brussels, 1974).
4. *Towards a new energy policy strategy for the European Community* (*Bulletin of the European Communities, Supplement 4/74*, June 1974).
5. *Towards a community nuclear fuel supply policy*, Com(74)1963 (Brussels, 1974).
6. *Alternatives au nucléaire: réflexions sur les choix énergétiques de la France* (L'Institut Economique et Juridique de L'Energie, Presses Universitaires de Grenoble, February 1975).
7. N. J. D. Lucas, 'Nuclear Power in the EEC – the cost of security' in *Energy Policy* (June 1976).
8. P. R. Odell, 'Europe and the Cost of Energy – Nuclear Power or Oil and Gas' in *Energy Policy* (June 1976).
9. T. W. Berrie, 'The economics of system planning in bulk electricity supply' in *Electrical Review, Vol. 181* (15, 22, 29 September 1967).
10. Private Communication, National Coal Board.
11. L. Grainger, *Energy conversion technology in Western Europe* (Phil Trans. R. Soc. London A. **276**. 527, 1974). Also private communication, N.C.B.
12. N. J. D. Lucas, 'Energy Carriers in Europe' in *Energy Policy* (March 1977).
13. *First Periodical report on the Community action programme for the rational use of energy and draft recommendations of the Council*, Com(76)10 (Brussels, January 1976).
14. *Study of the European market for industrial nuclear power stations for the mixed production of steam and electricity* (Industry series report 1975–8, Commission of the European Communities, 1975).
15. Leon Lindberg and Stuart Scheingold, *Europe's Would-Be Polity* (Prentice Hall, 1970).
16. See D. Swann, *The Economics of the Common Market* (Penguin, 1970), for an introduction to the theory of a customs union when resources are not perceived as finite.

V

Conclusions

The introduction to this paper claimed the intention to examine the nature of political control of the highly technical energy policy and to examine the conflict between long-term planning and the short-term preoccupations of politicians with their constituencies. However little the results may live up to this, it is as well to acknowledge the original intention and group the conclusions so that they evolve roughly from questions of long-term planning, through those of policy formation, to finish with some opportunities for furthering a common energy policy.

Long-term Planning

1. The development of energy policy in Europe has been determined to a large extent by the inaccurate assessment of the prospects for nuclear power made in 1957 and on which Euratom was founded. There is evidence that these optimistic assessments were accepted in part because they appeared to suit the political objectives of the partisans of European unity. The deleterious consequences of this initial vision were as follows:

(a) the failure to appreciate the future prospects for oil meant that the Community was unable to exploit this vast change in the infra-structure of energy supply to the benefit of European integration;

(b) the same failure and the inappropriate institutional structure devised meant that the Community lost all initiative for energy policy;

(c) the divided responsibility for energy in the institutional structure made it difficult to formulate a common policy and ensured much effort was diverted to inter-Executive struggles;

(d) distinct national differences in oil policy developed in the member states which are now difficult to eradicate;

(e) the failure of Euratom lowered the prestige of the Community;

159

(f) the Commission was left with an able, dedicated and under-used reservoir of nuclear talent which has been a permanent and persuasive pressure group ever since.

2. The foregoing impediments to the evolution of a common policy were reinforced by the remarkable success of the oil companies in providing stable supplies of oil at falling prices; this removed all sense of urgency up until about 1970/71. The oil companies in practice pre-empted the European vision and initiative which belonged in principle to the Commission.

3. The record of success of long-term planning of energy supplies in the Community has been disastrous. The consequences of the institutional structure set up in 1957 have been sketched; the good evidence available at the time that oil would be cheap and plentiful was ignored. By 1967 the predominance of oil was established. Warnings were heard that Middle Eastern oil might not always be cheap and secure, but the Commission devised a plan based on unrestricted imports; again it attempted detailed long-term planning, but ignored indications of gross change. A similar, but even more exaggerated, state of affairs pertained in 1972. In 1974 the Commission published plans for the future based on the historical growth of demand for electricity and ignored sound evidence that the market for electricity was beginning to saturate; again it attempted detailed planning for the future, but ignored indications of change. One cannot foresee the future; to plan in detail is absurd. It is much more important to identify the qualitative form of change and to design policies and institutions that will cope. The clear qualitative features of the future are that:

oil reserves are severely limited;

nuclear power is not a simple replacement and suffers heavy economic penalties in heating duties;

the proliferation of nuclear technology is a serious threat.

It follows that:

many resources must be put into developing alternative forms of energy supply, especially world-traded coal and coal processing;

the Community must adopt a serious conservation programme;

the Community must acknowledge the seriousness of the proliferation of nuclear weapons and make every effort to ensure the most satisfactory forms of control.

Policy Formation

4. The Community is in politics, not business. Ultimately, the nature of the energy policy one would like to see depends on one's attitude to

enhanced political unity. I believe that energy forms part of the whole question of who will take the decisions about the future of Europe. If they are taken by outsiders then that is a loss to Europe, because however friendly détente and however understanding dialogue may be, ultimately the realities of power prevail.

5. The three principal matters with which European energy policy should be concerned are: security of supplies in the short term; the development of secure and adequate supplies in the long term; and the political consequences of proliferation of nuclear technology.

Each of these three matters has a strong political content. The driving force for a common energy policy is, therefore, essentially political.

6. The lack of progress in a common energy policy since 1973 is a result partly of factors external to the Commission.

(a) There have been tensions between countries working on a dialogue between consumers and producers and those working on consumer solidarity; these tensions were present even in the Council of Ministers' meeting preceding the Washington Conference in February 1974.

(b) Member states faced with a crisis sought individual deals (especially the United Kingdom and France) and subsequently sought solutions outside the Community; effort was diverted from a common energy policy to the North-South dialogue, with little reward.

(c) The most successful initiative since the 1973 oil crisis has been the International Energy Agency, which has agreed an oil sharing procedure, a minimum support price for oil and joint projects for the development of new energy technologies. Partly because of a preference for the North Atlantic alignment and partly because of the success of the IEA, Germany and the United Kingdom have made it the focus of their activities in international energy matters. Because of the intransigence of France, and in no way through its own fault, the Commission has been cut off from the most effective existing institution.

But there are also reasons within the Community machine for the lack of progress:

(a) In matters like energy which are politically and technically complex there is no sustained political drive towards a common policy. Even if the periodic declarations by the European Council of a political will to form a common energy policy are genuine, the design of a suitable policy is a long and technical matter beyond the scope of either the European Council or the Council of Ministers. The bulk of arbitration on energy matters takes place in the High-Level Working Group of national civil servants; the national representatives are good negotiators, but by virtue of their functions

161

have little motive to make material concessions for the benefit of European ideals. Originally the political drive was intended to lie with the Commission, but as intergovernmental institutions have assumed responsibility for arbitration and negotiation, so the influence of the Commission has waned. There is certainly a large political input into the Commission's original constructions, but it has little influence at the level where complex policies are actually negotiated. The essential political incentives for a common energy policy, noted in section 5 above, are not effective in the places where the decisions are conceived. More frequent summit meetings and the creation of a political secretariat might help a little.

(b) The political sensitivity of the Commission has sometimes been used less to steer difficult measures through the Council than to detect the line of least political resistance. The Commission was led to do this by the revival of nationalism in 1964/65 and the clear signal that member states were more concerned with the domestic effects of policies than their suitability to Europe as a whole. The new, timid attitude of the Commission developed over the following 10 years and is now well established.

(c) The nature of the Community as a common market makes it easiest to develop policies for expandable resources, e.g. the customs union and agriculture. Countries with non-renewable or sensitive resources, like energy and fish, will not want unrestricted access by others to their resources; the philosophy of a common market is not, in these cases, enough. This fact does not seem to have been given due weight in framing proposals for common policies in energy.

(d) The technical basis of proposals, particularly those relating to nuclear energy, has been consistently unsound, leading to an exaggerated view of the prospects for nuclear energy and eventual undermining of the authority of the Commission in energy matters.

Substance of a Common Energy Policy

7. The Community should redirect its principal effort to the construction of a common energy policy. This does not mean a comprehensive blueprint covering all industries and eventualities; it simply means a number of measures taken in common, sufficient to demonstrate a degree of solidarity among the member states of the EEC. In the absence of any manifestation of a common purpose the participation of the Community in international conferences can have no meaning.

8. The observation that the political incentives for a common energy policy are strong, coupled with the fact that the complexity of the issues

precludes decisions being taken in places where these political incentives are effective, suggests that one way of proceeding is to simplify the issues. In the past the Community has often moved forwards by means of decisions relatively simple in form, but with far-reaching consequences that were not properly understood at the time. Their simplicity of form permitted them to be negotiated in the highest political institutions leaving national civil services to assess the consequences thereafter. Decisions with something of this quality include the initial formation of the Community, the direct elections to the European Parliament (the powers of whose members are not clear even now), and the decision to introduce 200-mile limits, which has given the Commission unexpected powers and authority. It is, therefore, worthwhile formulating a proposal with this quality within the energy policy. An appropriate candidate of considerable merit in terms of its intrinsic value to a common energy policy is the proposal for a Community Energy Agency. This would have no direct interventionist powers, but would have its own budget to finance research and development, energy conservation and alternative sources. The Agency would be financed by a tax on all sources of energy, including indigenous sources.

9. It is greatly in Europe's interest that an effective world trade in coal should develop. There are powerful European interests against importing coal. The Commission could encourage organizations with this function. It could make and publish detailed investigations into the availability in third countries of coal that might be imported. The study could include estimates of costs, and consideration of the active constraints if coal were to be imported under long-term contract as joint ventures between the Community, the producing country and appropriate mining organizations and/or oil companies.

10. The case for distributing energy almost exclusively, or even principally as electricity is weak. Gasification of bulk fuel (coal and fuel oil) has at least as bright a commercial future as the next generation of nuclear reactors. The Commission could analyse the relative prospects of gasification and nuclear electricity in terms of cost in final use, make proposals for research and development and indicate possible targets as appropriate.

11. The Commission could make and publish detailed studies of the optimum handling of the North Sea hydrocarbons province in the context of Europe. It could take the initiative in persuading the United Kingdom Government of the necessity of refining substantial quantities of North Sea crude in Europe.

12. The Commission could suggest terms under which the United Kingdom could conclude long-term contracts for the sale of crude oil in Europe which would provide security of supply for continental states and generate a positive net cash flow for the United Kingdom.

13. The Commission could make much more effort to encourage energy conservation. In this area it has some advantages over national governments. The indispensable preliminary is to create a Directorate of Energy Conservation within the Directorate-General for Energy and thereby remove the present conflicts of interest.

14. A Community Hydrocarbons Supply Agency should be set up with exclusive right to negotiate contracts for the importing of hydrocarbons. The Community, being the largest importer of oil in the world, would by this means exert enormous influence on the market.

15. Europe has been, and will be, a principal source of the proliferation of nuclear technology. The Commission should prepare proposals for the most rigorous control of the transfer of nuclear technology to third countries, including proposals that all irradiated fuel be reprocessed in regional centres under international control. It should try to obtain consent from member states to use this as a basis for a Community view which the Community would press internationally.

Appendix I

Approximate dates in the progress of European integration and the changing perception of energy supplies in Europe between 1951 and 1958.

April 1951:   ECSC Treaty signed in Paris.

February 1952:   ECSC abolished barriers to trade in coal and iron ore among member states.

March 1955:   *The Price of Oil in Western Europe* is published by ECE.

June 1955:   The Messina conference convened.

July 1955:   M. Armand's report *Some Aspects of the European Energy Problem* is published.

October 1955:   M. Monnet's Action Committee is formed.

January 1956:   Action Committee publishes first declaration on an Atomic Energy Community.

February 1956:   Interim report of *Relance* Committee debated in Brussels.

April 1956:   Final report of *Relance* Committee published.

May 1956:   Hartley report published by OEEC.

June 1956:   Report of *Relance* Committee adopted as basis for final proposals.

September 1956:   *Oil – the outlook for Europe* published by OEEC. M. Monnet's action committee publishes second declaration on Euratom.

November 1956:   Target for Euratom requested.

March 1957:   Treaties of Rome signed.

May 1957:   *Target for Euratom* published.

January 1958:   Rome Treaties take effect. *Europe's need for oil* published by OEEC.

Appendix II

Secondary Legislation in Energy Policy

There is no official classification of the secondary legislation of the Community into sectorial policies. This Appendix contains some of the more important secondary legislation with a bearing on energy.

In implementation of the Treaty of Paris the Commission can issue *decisions, recommendations* and *opinions*. In implementation of the Treaties of Rome, the Council and Commission issue *regulations, directions, decisions, recommendations* and *opinions*.

Regulations of EEC and Euratom: These are binding and take direct effect in the member states, without any implementing action by member states, who may, however, often have to supplement regulations in various ways, notably by making provisions for their enforcement. But the regulations as they stand take effect without any such action.

Directives of EEC and Euratom: Directives leave member states the choice of form and methods for their implementation. Organizations and persons within member states are not, therefore, directly bound by directives, but are bound by the national law implementing those directives.

ECSC Decisions and Recommendations: The distinction between directly enforceable and non-directly enforceable acts also applies in the ECSC, but there is no simple rule as to whether a particular ECSC instrument falls into one category or the other.

ECSC Opinions and *Recommendations of the EEC and Euratom* are not binding.

Regulations – European Economic Community

1055/72: on notifying the Commission of imports of crude oil and natural gas in excess of 100,000 metric tonnes – extended in 1974 to cover petroleum products.

1056/72: on notifying the Commission of investment projects of interest to the Community in the petroleum, natural gas and electricity sectors – covers refineries, oil and gas pipelines, oil and gas storage, thermal power stations, hydroelectric power stations, transmission lines.

293/74: on information for the establishment of comprehensive energy balance sheets for the Community. It requires member states to give to the Commission details of production of crude oil and natural gas; imports, exports, deliveries, arrivals and

166

stocks of refined products; imports, exports, deliveries, arrivals and stocks of natural gas; production, consumption and trade of electricity; stocks of oil and coal at power stations.

Decisions and Directives – European Economic Community

68/414/EEC: Directive imposing an obligation on member states to maintain minimum stocks of crude oil and/or petroleum products of 65 days' consumption.

68/416/EEC: Decision on the conclusion and implementation of individual agreements between governments relating to the obligation of member states to maintain minimum stocks of crude oil and/or petroleum products.

72/425/EEC: Directive amending 68/414/EEC, and increasing the obligatory stocks to 95 days.

73/176/EEC: Decision adopting a programme of research in new technologies for the EEC (use of solar energy and recycling of materials).

Decisions – European Coal and Steel Community

3/71/ECSC: Decision on Community rules for interventions by member states for the benefit of the coal industry. Sets out the permissible objectives of financial aid by member states to their coal industries, obliges member states to give information on the aid to the Commission and details procedures of examination and authorization by the Commission and the form aid may take.

65/72/ECSC: Decision implementing Decision 3/71/ECSC (above). It sets out a common form for presentation of the information required from industries before aid can be authorized – lengthy and complicated forms for various eventualities.

Index